My Daddy Never Died

Raquel M. Hanic

Queenship

PUBLISHING COMPANY
P.O. Box 220 • Goleta, CA 93116
(800) 647-9882 • (805) 692-0043 • Fax: (805) 967-5133
www.queenship.org

Library of Congress Number # 2006905235

Published by:
  Queenship Publishing
  P.O. Box 220
  Goleta, CA 93116
  (800) 647-9882 • (805) 692-0043 • Fax: (805) 967-5133
  www.queenship.org

Printed in the United States of America

ISBN: 1-57918-316-6

Cover Photograph by Angela Karapantos
Didier Photography, Ft. Wayne, IN

I dedicate this book to my late brother, Rudy Escobedo. This book is for you, and anyone who shares your struggles. My prayer would be answered if this book would bless just one soul. Then it has served its purpose. Rudy, you taught me so many things about life. You showed me how to use the gift of laughter, and the importance of humor. I always told you that you were special. In death we see just how special you truly were. Thank you for being my baby brother. I love you.

Rocky

Acknowledgements

A ll thanks be to God the Father, His son, Jesus and The Holy Spirit. Without each member of the Trinity I would still be in my cave. It was the love of The Blessed Mother who took me directly to her Son. The Son took me the the Father, who introduced me to the Holy Spirit. I could not have completed this work without the Grace of God. I have never claimed to be a writer, just a fighter. God was the one who lead me each and every step of the way.

Special thanks to all of the prayer warriors who prayed this book into existance. I love you, Jean, Laureen, Tammy, Michelle, Rogelia, and Steve. My husband has always believed in me, even when he did not understand me. He has loved me unconditionally. Thank you for being there for me in the darkest of times.

I want to thank my parents for bringing me into this world. My brothers and sisters who have taught me so much about life. All of my family, each and every one of you. All of you have taught me about love and family.

Father Phister who has been a father to me. Father Jim Sapp who kept my feet on the ground and taught me to keep it simple. Father Machado who taught me the importance of obedience and wisdom. Father Jim Livingston who taught me how to be gentle and loving. Father Kaycee who showed me that priests were people, too. Father DeGrandis who taught me about forgiveness, Father Peter Mary Rookey who taught me to pray for others, Father Sudac who showed me the gift of self-sacrifice and Father Johm Hampsch who was the Christopher Columbus of inner healing. Without all of you, many souls would still be in bondage.

Each and every priest has been a gift from my Heavenly Father. Without all of you I surely would have died. During these dark times when the media speaks about our priests, we need to love them. I am not going to say that what happened is fine. I will say the opposite; it is never acceptable when an individual is victimized. Not by anyone, including a priest.

Their own fathers, brothers, cousins, uncles and various individuals are hurting young children every day. This is a crime that must be stopped. We need to offer help for the wounded and rejected. We need to love them and show them the way.

God will heal through our priests. He will do some powerful things at the hands of His apostles. They are anointed to carry on the ministry of

Jesus. If we allow, God will use each one of them to assist us in life.

To those of you who have been hurt by a priest, I would like to say one thing. I do not understand exactly how you must feel. I do however understand what you have been left with. The pain, humiliation and shame. I want to tell you, all priests are not like the one who hurt you. In life we have good and evil. You cannot allow the evil that wounded you to keep you from the Church that can heal you.

I am certain it will be difficult. You will need to make the same decision. Forgive and allow the healing touch of your Father in you heart. It is never an easy thing. Healing and truth are very difficult. If you do not face the truth, you will be allowing yourself to be raped over and over again. With the Grace of Our Father He will help you.

Linda Schubert who assisted me with numerous editing suggestions. Without your help I would have given up. Thank you for being a wonderful woman of Christ. Claire Schaefer who spent many hours talking with me and giving me wonderful advice.

Sister Geraldine who showed the the beauty and love of the Blessed Mother. Thank you, sister, for your wonderful smile and laughter.

I also wish to thank each and every person who hurt me. Without these experiences I would not be as close to Jesus as I am today. My past caused me to run to the arms of a loving Father.

I pray God will touch every heart, that He will give you a desire to ask for a healing. I was so much like St. Mary Magdalene. Jesus delivered her from seven demons. She followed Him the rest of His life. St. Mary Magdalene was at the foot of the Cross. She was there for Him even unto death. She was not off hiding somewhere. She loved Jesus and stayed with Him until the end.

I want to spread this good news to all sinners who are just like me. I know there are so many more of you out there. I pray this will give you the courage to come out in the light. Thank you, Jesus, for the love You have for me. Thank you, St. Mary Magdalene, for the hope you have given me. Thank You, my Heavenly Father, for you mercy.

I want to be just like St. Mary Magdalene. I do not want to be off somewhere hiding. I want to be at the foot of the Cross. I do not want to tell the world about me. I want to tell you about Jesus!

Contents

Foreword

I write you today to recommend a gritty and compelling testimony of healing from childhood abuse, *My Daddy Never Died*, by Raquel Hanic. What makes this book especially important is that Raquel's journey to wholeness is also a journey of faith. She was not only restored emotionally, but experienced a deeper, more authentic spiritual revival. Your readers will greatly appreciate that Raquel found healing and hope within the Catholic Church, through priests, the Blessed Mother, and God's holy word. Step by step, she was led to a greater emotional, psychological and spiritual freedom, as she allowed herself to be led by God into a deeper embrace of truth. Filled with wisdom, courage, honesty, forgiveness and hope, Raquel's testimony truly has the potential to become a means of healing for others. If you are looking for a story of real life miracles, a story that many thousands of wounded souls can relate to and find hope in, a story of courage and faith, you will find it in *My Daddy Never Died*.

Fr. James Livingston

Raquel Hanic's book is a timely inspiration for thousands of our contemporaries. In the midst of her sufferings and trials, she profiles her courage, her determination and her faith in the Lord, to overcome every obstacle in her life.

This work is a true testimony and witness, a beacon of hope to many who have experienced devastating trauma in their families and in their past. May Raquel's book be a source of determination of courage and healing to generations.

In Our Lord and Our Lady,
Father Clement J. Machado

Endorsements

I am most happy and pleased to share a few thought about Raquel Hanic's book. The topic is one that has to be addressed and spoken about. This must stop and be exposed for the tragedy that it is and the lives that bear the wounds, in many cases for life. I am most pleased that you have decided to publish this book.

Many books tell a story, inspire, and provide information, and inspiration. I found this book to be all of these and more. It has come from the heart of a wounded person who is willing to share for the benefit of all that this may open their eyes ears and hearts to realize that the steps for recovery are many, but that they start with the first step. The honest witness that Raquel Hanic shares will give all readers not only a glimpse into the window of her heart, but the assurance that help is possible, and forgiveness, while difficult, is possible, and is in fact the first step to recovery. The writer is an honest, prayerful, and sincere person who shares her story to be of help to others. Her ministry is a spiritual and extensive telling of her story, which unfortunately, is the experience of many. I would highly recommend this to all.

Sincerely,

Sister Geraldine Hartke O.S.F.
Campus Ministry • 2701 Spring Street • Fort Wayne, IN 46808

Raquel Hanic is well known to me. I was her Spiritual Advisor when I was working there, in the States. She is a good Catholic; always with that burning desire to do it right; a strong and ardent devotee of the blessed Mother Mary; and one of the few who still find time, despite the seeming "crowded schedule" of the day, to visit and adore the Lord in the Blessed Sacrament. Personally, I admire her zeal and genuine effort to share her wealth of experiences through writing, and most sincerely and readily too, recommend her to you!

Rev. Kaycee McDonald (SMMM)
Wuerzburg, Germany.

The book, *My Daddy Never Died*, has been life changing for me. It took me on a journey of laughing, crying, meditating and deep inner healing. I could find myself personally relating in this easy-to-read book of the courageous, life transforming journey the Lord desires us all to take on. I discovered the Lord's healing touch in the depth of my soul, healing me and making me a new creature in His amazing love! I believe this book will reach out and touch so many who walk around just like Raquel and I did, feeling that we are damaged goods, rejected and unworthy of love. There are so many of us walking around wounded from life. I discovered God wants us healed more than we desire it for ourselves. I believe with my whole heart that this book will take you on a road to new hope, new strength and a new life. I have grown in my appreciation of the Church and the Lord's amazing grace. I can say, I once was lost, but now I'm found. Praised be Jesus!

Tammie S.

Introduction

For so many years I was in search of happiness and peace. I wanted to feel normal inside. Ever since I can remember I never felt good about myself. I had a past that was full of pain and ugliness. I was ashamed to ever let anyone know the real me. I did not even know who I was. I had so many masks; I could pretend all was well. From the outside it looked like I had it all together. All one would have to do was take a closer look to really see.

I was an alcoholic at the age of fifteen. I had a hard life. I did not kow how to love, or be loved. I was the biggest sinner around. I was full of bitterness, resentment, unforgiveness, and hatred. I was a very angry young lady. All you would have to do was to look at my face and see. I could never hide anything well. Or so I thought.

I grew up in a family of seven. My mother had 2 sets of twins and I was the oldest of the five. I had gone to a Catholic school for twelve years but did not really appreciate my faith and the gift the God had given me.

Children amaze me. They can have fun walking out the door. If a child experiences pain, sooner or later that child will stop smiling. The life will be sucked out of the child. This child will become angry. We will then wonder, what is wrong with my child?

Many of us are wounded individuals. We hurt so deep in our heart no one would ever know. We in turn hurt others, because of what we were taught or shown. The old saying is true, "The apple does not fall far from the tree."

We are the lepers of the 21st century. Society is uncomfortable around lepers. I was a leper for a very long time. I was molested as a child, lived in an abusive home. My father had died when I was fifteen. It was not long after that I was raped by two young men. All of these events had taken their toll on me. I would compare myself to St. Mary Magdalene. The comforting thing is that she was special to Jesus.

My story is not the typical conversion story. This story is about the truth. My story is for all of the Mary Magdalenes and the tax collectors. This story is for the lepers who are all still suffering in silence.

It is time for you to come out of your caves and let the love of Jesus Chirst touch and heal your hearts. Open your hearts to the Father who wants to heal His children.

In these pages I will attempt to share how God has healed my heart in such an awesome way.

I pray that all will be for the glory and honor of the Almighty. Because if you knew me then you would know, it was an act of God that I am here today.

It was the mercy of a loving Father who opened His arms to his prodigal daughter.

My dad always used to say to me. "Never forget where you came from". I pray that I never forget for one moment, it was Jesus who brought me out of my cave. And that I may never forget where I came from.

1

Those who honor their father atone for sins, those who respect their mother are like those who lay up treasure. (Sirach 3:3-4)

Where I came from

I was the oldest of five children. I have two brothers and two sisters, two sets of twins. I remember saying many times, "God knew what he was doing. The world could only handle one of me."

My family is very large; each of my parents had six brothers and sisters. My mother has siblings who are twins. I was surrounded by twins, and a lot of relatives. My only friends I had when I was younger were my cousins.

I inherited from my father the passion for Latin culture. I can get a bit too passionate. I was taught about the importance of family. My dad said, "Remember, blood is thicker than water."

I was the oldest grandchild and niece on both of my parents' sides. I was called, "Number One" so many times that I began to believe it. Still to this day, when I am introduced they say, "This is Raquel; she is the first grandchild of the family."

My great grandmother Amma would babysit. Because she could speak only Spanish we would tell my dad, "We could not understand what she was saying." This used to get us out of trouble and we used this excuse for as long as we could. Like everything we pushed it to the end.

The first time that I was molested was by a female babysitter. She made me promise to not tell anyone what happened. She promised me candy if I could keep the secret.

My mom came home and asked me questions about our day. She said, "What did you do when we were gone?" I answered, "We played and..." I stopped in mid-sentence. I looked at her and said, "Oh, I can't tell you or else she will not bring me candy the next time." Calmly she said, "If you tell me what happened, I will give you even more candy." With that I told my mom every detail.

The next thing I can remember is being in a car with my dad. I had gone with him many times before. Whoever went with him always got a treat. This ride was much different than the rest. We pulled up to a house I did not recognize. We walked up to the house, he knocked and a heavy set woman answered the door. She let us in and my dad started talking to her.

Moments later I saw a familiar face. It was the babysitter, our eyes met. At that moment she knew I had told our secret. The woman started yelling at her, crying all of the while. The young girl attempted to cover herself while her mother beat her. The young girl was crying and yelling. I was terrified and I just knew it was my fault. I wondered what she did to deserve this. Why did I ever tell? I never wanted to see anyone hit. This greatly affected me. I made an inner vow, promising I would never tell again.

Many times during my young life I was violated. This was the only time I would tell anyone. The only thing that I, as a young girl, could do was to bury it. I began to think that it was a normal, something that happened to everyone. I never talked about this to a soul. Deep in my heart I knew that it was wrong.

Each time, a part of my heart was ripped out. I was not sure what was wrong with me but I knew that something was. As the months turned into years, my personality began to become affected. I had always felt ugly and had a bad temper. I went from a happy, carefree young girl to an insecure, scared child. Something inside of me was changing; the light was growing dark. I kept all of the secrets locked in my heart for twenty-five years.

I was baptized a Roman Catholic. I attended Catholic schools for twelve years. All I ever knew was the Catholic Mass. Like so many others, I did not appreciate the true gift of the faith. I took it for granted, not truly understanding the gift of my faith.

When we were young, we moved into our dream house. It had an in-ground swimming pool in the back yard. My parents failed to tell us that they found witchcraft books in my bedroom. That should have been a sign that things were going to get bad.

At first things were great. These were the happiest years of my childhood. Carefree and happy; we had numerous family get-togethers, cookouts with all of the cousins, aunts and uncles. It was awesome; we enjoyed being together.

We took family vacations, Florida, Texas, Mexico, Toledo Zoo, Cincinnati Reds ball game, amusement parks, and just special times with the family. My favorite vacation was when we went to the Smoky Mountains. We spent a week in a log cabin enjoying nature and playing for hours in a stream that was down the mountain. On the way home my parents took us to Memphis, Tennessee to Graceland.

We all enjoyed holidays. There was not a Christmas I can remember without a visit from Santa. He would always stop by my grandparents on Christmas Eve. The amazing thing was that he knew all of our names.

Wedding receptions were always a good time. My family loved to dance. My grandmother and her brother could move with the best of them. I loved to watch them on the dance floor. My grandmother had some moves that many twenty-year-olds do not. I loved to dance with my dad. I was the happiest when my parents would glide to a slow song.

We were convinced that Sister Sledge wrote the song "We Are Family" for us. It was our song, it described us. Wherever we were, all of us would stop and come to the dance floor when this song was playing.

As a young girl I loved Elvis Presley. He was my idol. I had an old 45 record player my parents gave me. I had many singles of Elvis and would spend hours listening to music. I had just about every record that Elvis had made. I would sing right along with him. I enjoyed the time alone with no twins. This was my special time when I could pretend none of those things ever happened.

I was devastated when Elvis died. I felt like I lost a dear friend of mine. Little did I know that I would feel the same way that Lisa Marie did five years later. The king in my life would be joining Elvis.

My dad had decided to go into business with the family. We bought an old grocery store and converted it into a beautiful Mexican Restaurant, "La Casa Escobedo".

My dad was the evening bartender. That meant he would be gone more in the evenings. At first it was hard for us. We were used to him being around at night. He was our protector and our security. I would leave him notes on the back door. I would surprise him by making him his favorite sandwich. I loved my dad; I was a "daddy's girl."

Being the oldest, I learned to take care of the kids. I watched my younger brothers and sisters when my parents worked. I had major responsibilty at a young age.

It was not long before things started to change at home. My dad was gone more and the fighting increased. My father was getting angrier day by day. We used to watch him as he came in the back gate. We would study him to see what type of mood he was in. That way we would know what type of face to put on.

We all knew that he had a temper and were not going to be the ones to set him off. The financial burdens were coming down on him. My dad had the responsibilty of a family of seven and the pressures to keep the dream house. My parents worked so hard to give us all that they never had. It was taking its toll.

One Sunday, my mom had made a huge family dinner. We were all sitting down at the table ready to eat. The table was set and we were ready to dig in. All at once my dad got angry and started to yell. Before I knew it he picked up the table and threw it across the room.

Food and dishes were everywhere. The only thing that was left was the five of us. We were still gathered in a circle waiting for our dinner. That incident scared each of us. We were certain of one thing, we were not going to make my dad mad.

It was always worse when drinking was involved. I had a hard time sleeping at night, anticipating the mood he would be in when he came home. My bedroom was right next to my parents'. I could hear every fight that they had. Many times I would break into their room and stop the fights. If my dad would come in and go to sleep, I knew that it was okay for me to go back to sleep. This went on for years. I had become my mother's protector.

Amazingly, I was not afraid of my dad. He would never lay a hand on me. I never cried in all of the years. I never allowed myself to feel. If I cried, that meant that I was allowing myself to experience the pain. If I ever started to cry then I might not be able to stop.

The men in my father's family were taught to drink. It was normal; I mean real men drank didn't they? My family was full of what you might call "real men". Drinking was inherited and passed down from generation to generation. Today I can see that my dad had the same disease that I had. This disease brought so much destruction, on anything that was in its way.

I have no idea of the hurt my dad brought from his past. I can only guess that he was in pain because of his actions and the anger that was deep in him. There were many times he would come home late from the bar. We would all be awakened to hear about the barroom brawl. He would wake up with swollen hands and cuts on the back of his head.

Toward the end, he would come in my room and cry to me. One night in particular, he came in and knelt down next to my bed. He woke me up saying, "Raquel, I am so sorry for all that I have done to hurt you." I know that he realized all that I went through, he was sorry but had no way to control it. He was in a trap and he could not see a way out.

My dad had such a big heart. He taught us that we should not judge someone by their appearance. I can remember many times that he would hire people to do work at our house. Even though we were poor, he was always willing to help out those who were worse off than we.

The family finally had to make a difficult decision. They had to close the restaurant due to numerous reasons. My dad took this very hard. He lost all hope at this point. I know that it caused him so much pain. Our financial situation was getting worse by the day. Many times that big house with the pool had no electricity. We had our heat turned off more than once. The phone, and any other utility that could have been turned off, was at one time or another. This was very embarrassing for us. We would try to keep any friends that we did have away. We did not want anyone to know what was going on inside.

I can remember many times, during the coldest months of the winter, all huddled up in the living room. We would cover up and keep warm by the fire in our fireplace. It was a very sad and dark time in that house.

The big Christmases and the family vacations were a thing of the past. Things were definitely getting bad. We almost lost the house during these years. God sent one of His Shepherds to take care of us. The pastor from our Church came up with the money for us to have a place to live.

We had no medical insurance, and I got strep throat at least twice a year. I can remember being so sick. My mom would take me to the back door of the doctor's office. He would give us samples. We could not even afford the medicine.

I realized that something would happen in the house when I was sick. The fighting would stop. There was a time of peace. As a young girl I had all sorts of stomach problems. I would get these awful pains and feel sick to my stomach.

I ended up in the hospital and had to have surgery to have my appendix removed. My parents loved us and would only worry about us. So this was a good time for us. The problem is that I caught on to this. I enjoyed the time of peace so I began to pretend that I had an illness. This kept them busy and the house was still full of peace.

The financial pressures got to my dad and he attempted to make a living gambling. He thought that this could help the family. This meant that he would be gone more and come home late. When he won, we all knew it but we never heard if he lost. This only brought more trouble into the house.

The family could sense that things were not good. We were not talking about it. Kids were meant to be seen and not heard. We would remember what my dad told us, "What goes on in this house, stays in this house." We all kept up the silence. We were taught three things: don't talk, don't trust, and don't feel. I tried to pretend it was just a dream, and that it would be better the next day. That day did not come for a long time.

I lost my dad long before the day he died. The man everybody loved and who cared so much about his family, the man who would give a stranger the shirt off of his back, was slowly dying. What caused all of this to happen? Who or what stole my parents from us? The happy times were taken away. Was it the pain from his wounds? Was it alcohol? I was getting ready to follow in his footsteps. I loved him so much that I wanted to be just like him. For years I, too, lived with the pain from my past. Drowning the pain with alcohol and fighting anyone who would look at me. I guess I always felt it was destiny; I had to live up to my birthright. I was tough and angry. Inside, I had died as well.

2

May those who sow in tears reap with shouts of joy (Psalms 126:5)

The day my daddy died

These years were the most difficult for me. I was 15 the year my daddy died. It was Indian Summer and we were all grateful for the warm fall days. Even though my parents relationship was explosive at times, the last thing that I ever wanted was for him to die. I used to wish that they would get a divorce. That way the fighting might stop. But not for him to die. That was forever. I loved my dad.

The weekend before the accident was the first time that I drank alcohol. I was invited to go with a group of friends to a haunted house. I proceeded to get drunk for the first time. Unfortunately it was not the last, only the beginning. I finally had courage and self-esteem. Alcohol allowed me to be the person that I always wanted to be.

I had so much fun that evening. But the evening ended and I had to get home by curfew. I said a small prayer as I walked in the front door. Praying my father had already left for the evening. Many times over the past year, I begged him to stay home.

As I walked in the door he was getting ready to leave. I hurried up the stairs to get to my room. I did not want to get too close to him; I was afraid he might smell the alcohol. I was about half-way up the stairs when he called my name. "Raquel." I stopped and turned to my dad. Like a typical teenager I said "Yeah". He was silent, just studying my face. If he caught me I would never be able to leave the house until I was married. My father spoke next. "Did you have fun tonight?" Again my answer was the same. "Yeah."

I started to walk up the rest of the stairs to my room and once again he called my name. "Raquel." I turned to look at him again and he gave me a small smile and said " I love you." I said, " I love you too, Dad." I had finally made it to my bedroom where I quickly changed into my pajamas. I got in bed and waited to hear him leave.

I took a deep breath and was relieved that he did not catch me drinking

7

that evening. I did not get in trouble and I was free to go out again. But somehow I was sad. I disappointed him. I thought about all of the nights he would leave us and go to the bar. I guess in my own way I was getting back at him.

When I woke up the next morning I had such a terrible headache. It was not as much fun as the night before. I tried to hide this from my mom, which was not too hard with four other kids in the house.

I thought about the night before and how much fun I had. I could not wait to get to school to talk to my new friends. I finally had self-esteem. All I needed to do was to drink a few beers. That wasn't too bad.

I went to bed early that night. My hair was full of pink sponge curlers. I wanted to look my very best. I was excited to get to school, ready to talk to all of my new friends. About three in the morning I got up to go to the bathroom. As I walked past my parent's room I noticed my dad was awake. On my way back to my room he called my name. He began to talk to me. I remember all he said that early Monday morning.

"Raquel, always be a good person. Treat others the way you would want them to treat you. Do the best at everything you do." I agreed with him so I could get to bed. Then he said the one thing that caught my attention. " Raquel, never, ever, drink too much. It can and will cause you many problems." At this point he had my attention. I knew that he had caught me. The last thing that he said was "Never, forget where you came from."

I was silent and just listened to my dad. I started to walk away and told him good night. He called me back in and said, "Now come over here and give your dad a kiss goodnight." I smiled at him and gave him a hug and kiss. As he hugged me he told me, "Never forget that I will always love you." I told my dad that I loved him too. Then I went to bed and fell asleep.

Six o'clock in the morning came pretty fast. I did not want to get up. I was tired and it was Monday. My mom was in my doorway, as usual to wake me up.

Before I left for school, I did the one thing that I had been doing for the past six months. That summer I dreamt my father died. It was so real. This dream affected me deeply. It was so real and I was terrified he might die. Each day like clockwork, I would go in my parent's room. I would watch my dad sleeping, and made sure he was still breathing. I wanted to be reassured he was still alive.

The day my daddy died

So that day October 17th 1983 I did what I always did. And yes he was breathing. I could leave for school. All was good.

I was at school when I heard the news of my father. I was in Religion class when I was called out. My aunt was crying and I knew that something was definitely wrong. As we drove to the hospital she told me what happened. She said, " Your dad has been in an accident. He was pinned in his truck." I thought to myself. No big deal probably he broke his leg or something. I was not too worried.

In no way was I prepared for what was going to happen next. When we arrived at the hospital all of my dad's brothers and sisters were there. I noticed my mom. She was a wreck, crying so bad I could not figure out what was so wrong.

It was not long after that we were asked to come into a small room. The doctor wanted to talk to us. They had ran a few tests on my dad and he was going to explain the results to us.

The doctor started his conversation by saying, "I am sorry." Sorry, I thought for what? He explained that my dad's neck was broken from the hood of the truck. He was surprised that he had survived the impact. He added that my father must be a strong man. He explained that he was breathing on a respirator and that there still was some brain activity. There was nothing he could do for my dad.

I could not believe my ears. There was nothing that could be done for him. What did that mean? I could not take another moment of this. I ran out of that room, out of the emergency room entrance and across the street to the church. I needed help and it could only come from Him.

I went to the front of the church and headed straight to the altar. I kneeled down in front of the altar and prayed like I had never prayed before. I cried and cried. I begged God to spare his life. He was just 34 and had five kids to take care of. We needed him. I prayed the prayers of a child. I had already been through so much. I could not take this. I was certain God heard me. I knew my dad would make it.

The next week was a blur to me. I spent many days and nights at the hospital sleeping in the ICU waiting room. I did not want to leave. I was afraid that he might die. Many family members came to see my dad that week. Some traveled long distances. It was a difficult time for everyone.

I had spent many hours just sitting with him, late at night when everyone else was asleep. I had many talks with my dad. I begged him to pull through. I asked him to squeeze my hand if he heard me. I knew that he was going to make it. I was sure of it. God would answer my prayers.

Late one night I took off the scapular that had been given to me at my first communion. I wrapped it around my dad's hands. I could not put around his neck due to the brace that was around it. I remembered the promise Our Lady had given. "Who so ever dies wearing this scapular shall not suffer eternal fire." I wanted to make sure that my dad went to heaven. I was old enough to know. He did not go to church on Sundays or go to confession. And sometimes he was not very nice to us. I was concerned for his soul. I was sure that he would be spared if he had this scapular.

One week later I went back to school. I tried to pretend everything was normal. People were coming up and asking me questions I wanted to smile but found it very difficult.

It was late in the day when two of my aunts came to pick me up. We did not speak to each other. Nothing needed to be said. It was not until we got into the car that they told me the news. The hospital test showed no brain activity. We were going to say good-bye. The decision was made. They would turn off the respirator. At this point I could not cry. I was numb. Over the week I had come to terms with this. I knew that there was a chance but I still could not believe that my daddy was going to die.

On the way to the hospital many different thoughts ran through my mind. I could not bring myself to talk. I just stared out of the window. Thinking, "I could use a beer right about now." I did not want to feel the intense pain that was ripping my heart apart.

I was given a gift that many did not get before my dad's accident. I was able to tell him good-bye. I still thank God for this. He knew that I would need this from my daddy. When we finally arrived at the hospital, the waiting room was full of family members coming to say a last good-bye.

We were the last to go into the room, all of us, his wife and children. It was a very sad sight. We all looked at him alive for the last time. Even though he was mean at times to us, we all loved him. It tore us apart; this was it, the end. How do you tell someone that you love good-bye?

I just stood there holding my dad's hand. Looking at them, his hands had always been so big and strong to me. He did not look strong at this moment. This was the first time that I ever saw my father weak. Helpless, lifeless, he was not able to speak to us and tell us that he was sorry, that he was okay and we would be okay.

The day my daddy died

I did not stay in there long this time. Before leaving, I did the one thing that I had done so many times before. I stopped and looked at my dad. I watched him breathe for one last time. I left the room and my daddy. I walked though the ICU waiting room for one last time. I waited in the hall.

It was not long after when my mom walked through the doors and tears were streaming down her face. I knew that it was over. My daddy had lost the battle. On October 24th 1983 my daddy died.

After the funeral we walked back into that big brick house. It was so different. He was never coming back. He was gone forever.

3

A few days later the younger son gathered all he had and traveled to a distant country, and there he squandered his property in dissolute living. When he spent everything, a severe famine took place throughout that country, and he began to be in need. (Luke 15:13-14)

Adolescent Years

After my dad's death I went crazy. I was full of so much pain I could not take it. I was drinking every weekend and fighting anyone who looked at me wrong. I had so much anger in me; this was the only way to get rid of it. Drinking was the only way that I could smile. I hated life, all that it had dealt me. I had no idea how to make myself feel better. I would try to smile but I felt nothing. My heart was getting harder and harder.

My family started to fall apart. We had no money and my mom had many hospital bills. I even started to drink during the week. I was out of control and no one could reach me.

Many times I asked God why He did not take me instead of my dad. If it would have been me, people could still go on. My mother, brothers and sisters neeeded my dad. I thought that God had made a terrible mistake.

I cried all the tears that were in me. It was during this time that I made promises to myself. I vowed to never love anyone else again. It hurt too much. I repeated this to myself so many times. I would not let anyone get too close to me; that way I could never be hurt again.

Life had to go on and it did. It did not seem fair. It was as though time should stop. But it didn't. The holidays were very tough, especially the first year after he died. It was a time for celebration but we were not celebrating this year. There were no traces of him left, just the memories and what was in our hearts.

My mom needed to go back to work. There were five children to think of and to pay for. It was difficult for us to adjust. My mother would need to spend more time at work and we were lonely. Yet in a strange way we were all free. He wasn't there to control us any longer but the trade-off was not

12

worth it. We missed him and wondered what would happen to us.

The summer after my father's death, my friend asked me to go with her to Purdue for a long weekend. I was so excited about going. I had never visited a college before and could not wait to get there. The idea was to go to college parties and get drunk, no adult supervision.

We attended our very first college party, nothing but drinking and dancing. It was great. I do not even remember when we finally came home. The second night we attended another party.

As the night wore on I continued to drink. I started to get bored and wanted to go back to the dorm. My friends wanted me to wait. I told them, "I will be fine." I started walking by myself. I felt no fear. Nothing could happen to me. My name was Rocky, and I was tough.

I came to an isolated area full of trees. Someone came up behind me. I was grabbed and thrown to the ground. It was dark and I could not see. Everything happened so fast. I did not even know what hit me. One guy was holding me down and the other began to rape me. I was fifteen years old and a virgin, not after this night. I was helpless. My strength was nothing compared to the two of them.

I screamed but no one could hear. All I could do was cry. It was like a terrible nightmare. I kept hoping it would be over and I would wake up at any time, but it wasn't a dream. I heard yelling. When I looked up, I saw familiar faces. It was my friends. They helped me up and we returned to the dorm room.

We went back to the apartment and we waited for my friend's sister to come home. When she did, we told her what had happened. She was angry and told us that we could not tell anyone what happened. She looked at me and said, "You know that you wanted it." I could not believe what she had just said to me. How could she say such a thing? The last thing that I ever wanted was to be raped. I would be silent like all of the other times. I knew how to keep a secret.

I did not want to leave the apartment for the rest of the time that we were there. I was so embarrassed and ashamed, I blamed myself. I should not have walked alone. I felt dirty and that everyone that looked at me could see what had happened. This was just one more thing that caused my heart to break. It seemed that only bad things happened to me.

On the way home my friend asked me again not to tell. I did not want anyone to know about this. I would definitely not be talking about it again. Inside I just wanted to scream. I wanted to cry. I wanted my dad, he could fix it.

This was not how I pictured my first time. I wanted it to be on my wedding night. I wanted to get home so fast. I needed to see my mom. I would be safe at my own home in my own bed.

When we pulled up there were many cars at my house. As I walked in the back yard I realized something was wrong. I had seen these looks before. All of my mother's family was there. They were all crying. My unlce died the evening before. I would never be able to tell my mom what happened to me. She had already been through so much.

So much had happened over the last six months. My dad had died, my mom went back to work, I was raped and now this, my uncle died. What else could happen to a family?

During this time I became an anorexic. I hated everything about me. It was my way of punishing. Once I started, I could not stop. I could go without food for days. I was losing weight myself, which was a plus. My friends started to notice my weight loss. They were concerned and would talk to me about my problem. I took their concerns as compliments. I would think, "They are just jealous." This behavior lasted for two years. My only food was beer and uppers. It is a miracle I lived through these years. My guardian angel was very busy.

Graduation time had come and so many things were going to change. The ceremony was so hard for me. I always pictured my dad there with a smile on his face. Many of my friends were off to college, but not me.

During this time in my life I drifted away from God. I did not want anything to do with Him. I blamed Him for allowing all of this pain to happen. I did not go to church anymore. I just kept sinking deeper and deeper into my pit of hell.

Many of my high school friends were coming home for a visit. We planned on going across the state line to Ohio where the legal age to drink was 18. I would drive. A night at the Palace was always a good time.

I had drunk as much as normal. All of us had plenty to drink, so I would be the one to drive. I did not think I was in bad shape.

It was not long after I got on the road that I was pulled over. I saw flashing lights in my rear view mirror. I was looking around to see another car that they wanted to pull over. There was no other car, just mine. I quickly put a penny into my mouth. I had heard that if you sucked on a penny, the breathalizer test would come out ok.

The first thing that the cop asked me was the same old question. "Have you been drinking?" I looked up at him and quickly answered "Yes, sir just a few beers." I was then asked to walk a straight line. I had failed; I said to the officer, "It must be the boots I am wearing. I lost my balance." He then asked me to recite the alphabet backwards. No one could do that. I was being set up.

I was told that I would need to go to the police station for a breathalizer test. I was terrified. What would happen to me? What would my mom say?

Upon arriving at the station I was escorted to a small room where I was asked to blow into this machine. I took a deep breath all the while trying to hold it so very little air would make it to the machine. I failed the test, and started cyring.

I then had to make the call to my mom. I was crying so hard she could not understand a word that I was saying. One of the officers had to get on the phone and explain to her what was happening. He told her that I would need to spend the night in jail.

I could not run this time. As much as I wanted to, I was trapped. Locked down, the only place I could go to was a small cell.

I was kept in the drunk tank for the night. When I woke up my head hurt so bad. I did not know where I was. It wasn't long after I opened my eyes that I remembered all that happened the night before. I did not belong here. Jails are for criminals. I was not a criminal; I just had a little too much to drink. What's so wrong with that?

My mom came to visit me. Tears started to stream down my face. All I could say was "Get me out of here." She just looked at me and told me. "I can't, Ohio law says that you have to spend three nights in jail for drinking and driving." I looked at her shocked. I wanted to go home, to get as far away from here as I could.

That afternoon I was moved to the women's cell block. I was sure that I would be beat up by some biker chick. I just sat in my cell not wanting to talk to anyone. We were told when we could take a shower and the bathroom was right in the middle of the cell. I stayed in my cell.

By the second day, a few of the ladies started talking to me. At first my answers were short. They asked the normal questions. "What are you in for?" I would answer their questions, and being polite, I asked them the same question. I was this little girl who went to private schools. I did not belong here. Or did I? They all had a story: one was in for prostitution, another for check fraud, and there was an older woman who was there for drinking and driving.

The day had finally come for me to go to court. I was going home and I could not wait to call all of my friends. I wanted to sleep in my own bed.

The courtroom was full. I saw my mom and was grateful she was there. My name was finally called. I approached the judge with handcuffs on. I had been praying so much over the past days. I needed a miracle.

The baliff read the charges that were filed against me. The judge looked at my mom and started asking her a few questions. "Have you been having any other problems with her?" She told him of my drinking and the late nights. He was silent, looking at the two of us. He took a deep breath and said something I never expected. "Well, I have never done this before. I am going to order that your daughter complete an inpatient treatment for drug and alcohol addiction." I was shocked. He looked at us and said, "I hope this helps you, young lady."

The drive home was long. We stopped home for a few clothes and went to the hospital. We spoke with a counselor and it was decided I would be admitted. I would be spending the next 28 days in treatment.

The program consisted of meetings, group therapy, and individual counseling sessions with the alcohol counselor. I said good-bye to my mom. This was the longest amount of time that I had ever been away from my family.

I could not believe all that had happened over the past week. I would be stuck here with total strangers for 28 days. I was angry at my mom for leaving me there. I guess that this was tough love. I put my mom through some very painful and difficult times. For that I am deeply sorry. I pray that she has forgiven me.

I was given medication for withdrawls and sent to my first meeting. I looked at the ground the whole time. I heard many stories that evening. Some were very sad. All of the people in this treatment program were addicts. Some to alcohol, marijuana, heroine, cocaine. It was extremly intimidiating. All were different colors and backgrounds with one thing in common. They were all addicted to something or another. I did not believe I was an alcoholic. I could stop anytime that I wanted to.

I started to casually talk to this man named John. He seemed to be nice enough. One evening, after the group session, I started to back to my room. I could sense that I was not alone. John pinned me against the wall. I could not even scream. But just as quickly as it all happened another man from our group was there. He pulled John away from me and threatened him with his life. Bill told John "If you come near her again, I will kill you." I was so grateful for his help.

This incident began what I thought was a friendship with Bill. I I felt safe for the first time, since the death of my father.

Bill and I spent many hours talking. I was very young and naïve. He gave me his telephone number in case I had a hard time when I got out. I also gave him mine just in case. I never intended to use it, but just to be safe.

I was released and determined to not drink. It had been over a month since I had seen any of my friends. The one thing that we had in common was partying. Now what would we do?

Everyone looked at me differently. It was not the same. I did not fit in anywhere. I was living in a strange house and my friends didn't even want to talk to me. I was sinking deeper and deeper into depresion.

Soon after I came home, I got a phone call from a friendly voice, it was Bill. He invited me to go to a meeting with him. I wanted to talk to someone who understood me. I didn't tell my mom who I was going with and she agreed to let me go.

My mom did not approve of this friendship. I could not understand her. Eventually Bill and I started to have a few beers. He was in treatment for heroine. His excuse was, "I do not have a problem whith alcohol." He looked at me and said, "You are not an alcoholic." He convinced me and I started to drink again.

I was sneaking out of my house to meet him. My mom was going crazy. I was drinking again every day. We became more than friends. I never felt right about it, but, had no one else to talk to.

My mom had gotten tired of all the problems. She gave me a choice, either I stop this friendship with Bill or I would need to find another place to live. There was no choice for me. I needed to have at least one friend. So I left home

Bill had offered to pay for an apartment for me, I accepted. It was not in a great part of town, directly across from a bar. Late at night you could hear the fights that were taking place. Each night I would tremble from the fear.

I was not talking to my mom, my family or any of my friends. It was during there lonely times that I started to pray. I would pray Hail Mary after Hail Mary. I did not know what else to do.

Bill had taken my tax return and my check book. He wrote bad checks and I was left with the debt. I knew that my family would not give me money. They thought that I was on serious drugs.

One evening Bill showed up and told me to get ready. I asked him "Where are we going?" He did not answer me. We were driving for at least fifteen minutes in silence. Again, I asked him the same question. "Where are we going?" He just looked straight ahead. "To a friend's house." I asked him, "For what?" Finally, he told me "You are going to have sex with him and he is going to pay me." I could not believe my ears, "What did you just say?" All of the anger that I had in me came out that evening. I looked at him with rage I said to him, "That will never happen. You will have to kill me first. I will need to be dead for you to ever get me to do that. So Bill, you better kill me."

He must have believed me, because he turned the car around and took me back to the apartment. We did not speak another word. I knew that I had to get very far from him and fast. Who knows, he might take me up on that offer and kill me.

What upset me the most was that everybody was right about him. I was so blinded by all of the games he played. The past five months were the lowest in my life. I never felt so alone. I was a perfect target for such a game.

The next day I tried to call my mom, but she was not home. I did not know what to do next or who to call. I just stood there at the payphone, waiting for a miracle.

It was then that I head a car horn. I tried to ignore it, but again I heard the sound of the horn. I then heard someone yell out my name. No one that I knew would be in this part of town. I looked up to see a woman who used to work with me at a restaurant. I was grateful to see someone friendly at this point. I told her that I had an apartment across the street. I invited her up to see it. We talked about all that happened to me over the past eight months. I cried as I told her the details. She just listened to me.

When I was finished she looked straight at me and said, "I am moving into a house, would you like to be my roommate?" I did not have a job or a way to get there. I thanked her for the offer, and explained her situation. She smiled at me and said "We are hiring waitresses where I work; I will put in a good word for you." It was settled, she would take me to apply for the job, and if I was hired, we would work the same shift.

Within a week I had a job and a new place to live. Things were looking up for me. I started working and was talking to my family again. I know

Adolescent Years

that they did not trust me very much. At least I had a job and was away from Bill. Things started looking up for me.

I knew that I had to get my life in order. Somehow things needed to turn around for me. I had to start over. I was determined to become a respectable person. I knew that it was not going to be easy, but afterall my name was Rocky. I had always been a fighter. I still had plenty of fight left in me. I was a survivor and that it what I intended on doing.

4

He set off and went to his father. But while he was still far off, his father saw him and was filled with compassion; he ran and put his arms around him and kissed him. (Luke 15:20)

Return of
the prodigal daughter

Things had started to get better for me on the outside. I loved my job as a waitress. I enjoyed talking with people. I was in my element. I started to feel like I was a normal person. Finally I was able to contribute to society.

I met my husband Steve when we were sophomores in high school. We lived in the same part of town, but hung around different people. He attended the public high school.

Steve has always said he fell in love with me the first time we met. I, on the other hand, did not. I was a tough young girl and was not about to get too close to anyone.

A friend of mine invited me out for an evening of fun. Steve would be joining us. He agreed to buy the beer and cigarettes. The best part of it was the free beer.

We started out by playing a drinking game. I seemed to be the target. Before I knew it, I woke up on someone's bed. It was dark and I was all alone. My friend had left me. I was so upset. I had to work at 6:00 am. I could not lose my job. It was the only good thing I had at this point.

I made it home in just enough time to get ready for work. I was exhausted and knew what I needed to do to get ready for the long day ahead of me. I popped a 357 Magnum. It would take about an hour before I had the energy I needed to make it through the day.

Steve called and invited me out for dinner. Against my better judgment I said yes. The evening went better than I expected. We enjoyed our time together. He was easy to talk to. Steve was very gentle. I felt safe with him from the first date. I told him all I could about the past eight months.

After opening up to him, I looked straight at him and said, "At this point you do not mean anything to me. I am sure I do not mean anything to you. If you can not handle everything I just told you. I understand I know it is a lot to handle. I will get over it and so will you. I want you to know the truth. If you do not want to go out again, that is fine with me." I was completely surprised by Steve's reaction. He looked at me and said, "It does not matter to me what anyone says. I enjoyed our time together." I was relieved that he said this. I was not sure anyone would have anything to do with me.

From that time on we spent so much time together. We would spend many hours talking and laughing. We did have one thing in common. We both liked to drink beer. When we first started dating I could drink him under the table. I was eighteen and had been an alcoholic for three years. I would not get sick to my stomach. I could drink with the best of them, and did for years. It was mostly beer, but I would switch to a shot when the beer did not taste too good.

Steve and I had been dating for about two months and we decided to move in together. It just made sense. During these times we talked about getting married. That was something that came up over and over again. I could think of being with no one other than Steve.

Shortly after we moved in together I found out that I was pregnant. We decided to keep the baby. We were young, but that is what we wanted. He proposed and I accepted. We were going to get married in October.

We had talked to both of the families and started to prepare for the wedding. We were young and in love. Nothing else mattered. We were going to have a baby and live happily ever after.

We got married at the same church I had been to so many times. It was the church I ran to when I begged God to save my dad, the same church where my dad's funeral had been almost three years to the date. The strange thing about Steve was that his birthday was the same day my dad died. That, to me, is not an accident.

The day came when Steve and I would get married. My family was emotional. The pain in our hearts was still there. It was a happy day but also a sad day. My grandfather walked me down the aisle. I wanted the closest thing to my dad; after all he was his father. My mom was crying; all sorts of thoughts must have been running through her mind. I had had so many difficulties over the last three years. She could rest a bit knowing I would be taken care of. I am sure she prayed that her first grandchild would be taken care of.

We walked up the stairs and stood at the back of the church. As I looked down the long aisle, memories flooded into my mind. I could still see the casket in the middle of the aisle. I could not run from it. I had to walk around it to get to Steve.

We had so many dreams, dreams of the perfect life and the perfect family. We had no doubts, not like everyone else. The time had come when we were saying our vows. The two of us and God. He was there and was going to help us to stay together no matter what.

Jesus was fully aware of the beginning we both had, all of the wounds and the pains. He knew all too well. Father said, "What God has joined together, let no man separate." Man has tried to separate us. At times we both have, but God has not allowed this to happen.

Our first daughter was born and we were happy just spending time together. We were living a simple life and were content with it. Steve wanted me to stay home with the baby. I did for a while, until she was eight months old. I wanted to do something to help him.

I started working various jobs. I was hired to work as a telemarketer for a large cooperation. This was my first taste of the corporate world and I loved it. This job did not last long and I was back to square one.

I worked as a customer service manager. This was the job that gave me the experience I needed. It also gave me much more than I had bargained for. I was about to enter a world of drinking and craziness that would bring all sorts of problems into the marriage.

I was exposed to colorful individuals with various back grounds. At first I was very intimidated; they all scared me. It did not take me long to feel comfortable. Rocky had to come out many times during those years.

There was not one person I met that did not drink. My drinking during these years picked back up. I had gotten to the point where I would drink every day. I would try to tell myself that the job was too stressful and I needed to calm down. It was not that hard to convince my husband. We had been drinking together on and off again over the past several years.

I would have parties at my house. I opened the door to the devil and invited him in the home. During these years the job, and all it gave me, was more important than my husband. I expected him to understand that I had friends who were males. The whole time I was so blind, I could not even see what damage I had done to the marriage. My temper was out of control. There were many days that I would just wake up angry. There was nothing that I could say I was mad at. I was just pissed off and hated myself during these years.

I just wanted to live my life and to not feel bad. I was looking to all sorts of ways to bring me happiness.

Today I see all of my choices greatly affected my husband. I hurt him so many times over the years. All of the time he just wanted me to love him the way he did me. I remember him saying this to me. He said, "Do you love me as much as I love you?" I would always answer yes to that question. I did not know what else to say to him. My heart was so hardened I could not possibly love him like he did me. I did not even know where to begin.

So, I did what I have always done. I kept silent, not allowing him to come into my heart.

That is how it has always been. I began to think I had a problem. I needed help, it just seemed too big. I started to search for peace and healing. I had read self-help books and was beginning to be exposed to forgiveness. I had a mountain of hardness that had been covering my heart. Little by little, things started to move in my life.

It was during this period of time I was exposed to New Age. It brought all the promises I was in search of. It spoke of God, so I thought it was good. I was not at all rooted in my Catholic faith. I had nothing to compare this to. I was sure this was my answer, so I went for it.

I am not an expert on New Age and the dangers of it. I will only tell you that I had more anxiety than ever before. New Age spoke about self. You have the power to heal yourself. It attempts to convince you that there is no devil, that way you have nothing to worry about. It is extremely dangerous.

My search and my involvement in New Age brought me right back to the truth. It took me back to my roots. It took me back home, to God, Jesus, Our Lady. It took me back to what I was taught as a child.

I had a deep desire to go back to church. I wanted to go to a Catholic church. Nothing to me was as important as going to Mass on Sunday. For the longest time when I went to Mass, all I would do was cry. Each and every Sunday I would have tears streaming down my face.

I felt so unworthy to be there. I could not go to communion; I needed to go to confession. I was not even ready for that. I just wanted to be in church. This went on for months. In my heart I knew it was my answer, my help, my salvation.

I was at the point where my body would shake until I was able to get a drink. I would tremble until I had at least four beers. After that I would feel better. Little did I know that I was physically addicted to alcohol.

Many times Steve would take care of me when I had too much to drink. He would protect me at all costs. If we were at a bar and I needed to get out, he would make sure I got home safely.

I have no idea who was responsible for me coming back to church. To all of you I say, thank you, and thank God. He heard your prayers and was getting ready to bring me home.

My aunt went to a place called Medjugorje in 1994. She came to our house to tell us all about the trip. She told us of the Blessed Mother appearing to six children in Europe. I was fascinated by all she said and just knew it was true. I wanted to go. I wanted to be close to The Blessed Mother and feel her. Before my aunt left, she gave me a rosary and a bottle of Holy Water. I thanked her and put the rosary away in my drawer. I turned to Steve and said to him, "Someday I want to go to Medjugorje." He smiled at me and said, "I will send you there one day, I promise." I left it at that and was grateful for the little peace I felt in my heart.

This was the beginning, the prodigal daughter had returned. She had gone out in the world and experienced it. She had tried all it had to offer. By the time it was all said and done, the prodigal daughter was eating with the swine. She was home and did not feel like she deserved to be in the house with her Father. You know the story. The father dropped what he was doing and ran to the child. He celebrated and had a party. His lost son had come home. This is what my Father did for me. He was so patient and gentle with me. He was there waiting with open arms for me to come home.

I have said many times that it was not God who left me; it was I who left him. I had wanted to have nothing to do with him. I needed to be on my own, to try things my way. I had a plan and it did not work. My life was worse than before.

It was terrible and I felt hopeless. I had nothing else I could do. I needed the Father, and prayed He would not turn away from me and punish me for all I had done.

It is true that His mercy endures forever. I am a living, breathing witness to this. I am a testimony to not only His Mercy, forgiveness, but also His love. I had thought that my life was exciting when I was out there drinking and carrying on. Little did I know just how exciting it was about to get.

5

Enter the narrow gate; for the gate is wide and the road is easy that leads to destruction, and there are many that take it. For the gate is narrow and the road is hard that leads to life, and there are few who find it. (Mathew 7:13-14)

The Journey begins

A ttending Mass each Sunday was emotional. I could feel the love of God. This kept me coming back week after week.

I was still drinking at the time. I was afraid of life without my crutch. I had gotten so used to the hangovers and the excuses. It was just a part of my life now. I was more afraid of life without drinking than I was of what I did while drinking.

I would hear this small voice saying, "Quit drinking." I would ignore it and push it away. There were even times when I considered it. That lasted only for a few hours. The voice never went away. It would always come back with the same words.

My marriage was in trouble. The years of my bad attitude and negativism, had created a wall between my husband and me. He was going out more and more. This was causing us to fight more than ever.

I had been working on forgiveness for about a year. I was making progress but had not gotten there quite yet. I still had so much work ahead of me. It seemed like I was climbing uphill. I had no self control, and would never admit when I was wrong. I was becoming a little nicer but had so far to go.

I was angry and sometimes downright mean. I was controlling and wanted to have things my way. With me there was no compromise.

My husband had tried for years to make me happy. He did everything he could, but it didn't work I was miserable on the inside.He attempted to buy me material things to keep me happy, but the happiness was always short-lived. He could not understand me. I hurt him by my actions. I caused him to feel rejected and made him feel that he was not good enough. I remember him saying to me, "I will never be able to make you happy."

I could not understand why he would say those things. I was not good company. I was not the good in wife Proverbs.

The seeds I had planted over the years were starting to sprout. It was awful. I, of course, would not take the responsibility. I blamed my circumstances, my job, my husband. I blamed everything for my mess except me.

There was so much silence and tension. You could cut it with a knife. We both had never wanted a divorce, we lived in homes without our fathers. We were holding on by a thread. At this point anything could come and cut it. It would not have taken too much.

My bottom came when I thought he would leave me. I was faced for the first time with the possibility that he may want out. I was beside myself. For the first time in my life I was afraid. I was afraid he may find someone else. I never thought the possibility existed. It was unheard of. I mean, Steve leave me?

I finally quit the job working with the subcontractors. I went to work for a corporation. I was attending church and expecting everything to just go away. I was expecting perfection and miracles, which I might add were not coming. I figured that God had not heard me yet.

As with all alcoholics, we do not quit unless we hit the wall. We will not just wake up one day and stop. It was going to have to be a huge wall, which I could not climb over. I was not going down without a fight.

I was alone one evening and started drinking. It was not long before all of the pain started to surface. I was attempting to hold back the tears. This was the night that God broke me. I started to cry and could not stop. I felt alone and that no one understood me. I needed to talk to my mom.

When I heard her voice, I cried even more. She could not recognize me. My mom was frantic. I said to her, "Mom, I can not take it anymore. It just hurts too much. I want to die." This sent fear rushing down her spine. She wanted to come and pick me up. I would not let her. I did not want her to see me like this. "No mom, I am fine. I am not going to kill myself. I just wish I would die." I sat there on the phone and cried tears, big, full tears.

Many of us alcoholics and addicts come to the point where death seems to be the only way out. For us there seems to be no hope. I was able to convince her, I would not hurt myself. She agreed to let me stay home, if I promised her to call in the morning.

I sat in the chair, not wanting to finish the beer I had just opened. I knelt down on the ground and prayed. I prayed like I never had before. I said, "God, if you are up there I need you. I am in trouble and need you like never before." I did not feel any different, so I got up and went to bed.

When I woke up the next morning I had this overwhelming desire to stop drinking. I wanted nothing to do with drinking ever again. I could see all of the problems it caused me. Every problem in my life was because of drinking. Finally, I was ready to give it up.

I do not know what happened the night before. My heart must have been in the perfect condition. God came in and He took over. All I had to do was put one foot in front of the other. He came in swiftly and quickly. I thank Him for that night even today. At that time, I had one leg in hell and the other on earth. I was in serious trouble. I knew the only answer for me was God.

Both my husband and I decided to quit drinking. It made life easier for both of us. At the beginning it was not that hard for me. I was determined and had made my decision.

We became pregnant with our third daughter about two months later. This made remaining sober even easier. I was ready to have a great life. I was finally willing to do whatever it took.

I started going to family rosaries. The Blessed Mother took me by the hand. She was the one who led me to Jesus. Through praying the rosary she brought me back to the Sacraments. I have later learned that one of the fifteen promises is, to destroy vices that take us away from God. She was the one who prayed for me to be healed from the alcoholism.

My prayer life started to expand. I started to read the lives of the Saints. I was being exposed to a totally different life, a good life, one of hope and a future. I wanted to have a better life, and dove in head first.

I learned about the Divine Mercy Chaplet and prayed this one daily. It was easy to remember and short. I was in need of His Mercy. I was the sinner He was talking about. I prayed for my family to be healed. I wanted the perfect family and was going to make it all happen. I stormed heaven with all of my requests.

The funny thing that happened was, I was changing, slowly, but I was changing. I wanted to be a better person. I wanted to be kind and patient. God began to deal with me and then to heal me.

I learned about St. Benedict. The one thing that caught my attention was that St. Benedict was used to keep evil away. I was having all sorts of experiences. I added St. Benedict to my list. Each night I would pray, "God, I ask you to allow St. Benedict to come into my house. Both inside and outside, keeping all evil away."

An amazing thing happened. While joining a family rosary, I met a man. We talked and prayed together. After we were finished he reached into his pockets and pulled out a medal. He said, "This is the St. Benedict medal. It will be for your protection." I looked at him in shock. I said, "I have been praying every night. I ask God to send me St. Benedict. I can not believe this. He did. God sent me St. Benedict." St. Benedict was not only in my house, but always with me. He was around my neck. St. Benedict and I would always be friends.

I started to sleep with a rosary in my hand. I did not want the Blessed Mother to be too far from me. The Blessed Mother was helping me day after day. I could feel her love. She was there so much in the beginning.

July 11th is a special day for me. It is the feast day of St. Benedict. I had been praying the rosary for about six months. The Blessed Mother was leading me to Confession. I had not been for twelve years. I wanted to go, but was terrified. I did not know what to expect. I was starting to have a deep sorrow for my sins. My heart was being softened, and I wanted to get all of the junk out.

My fear was bigger than my desire to go. After Mass on that July 11th I sat in the pew. I wanted to pray a bit before I left. I was talking to St. Benedict and thanking him for his prayers. I said to him, "Do you know what would make this day perfect? If I could go to confession." A priest came out and looked me straight in the eyes. He said, "Do you need confession?" I looked like a deer in the headlights. My eyes had to be as big as silver dollars. All I could say was, "Yes Father, I do." I went to confession for the first time in twelve years. I cried the entire time. I could feel the Mercy and Love Jesus has for us. It was awesome; I still thank St. Benedict for this.

Many times at Adoration I had a desire to go to confession. Jesus was always there to provide a priest for me. You can not tell me, God does not want to give sinners Mercy. He was going overboard. I have grown to love the sacrament of Confession. If we would only realize the true gift we have. Confession is such a beautiful thing.

Instead of being a regular at a bar, I became a regular at the neighborhood confessional. I would go in the confessional angry and come out calm. I could spend so long talking about the gift of confession. It is because I love it so much but will finish with this last story.

I had just finished reading a book about St. Pio. I loved it, he seemed to be tough. I had read about many times when he would not absolve a sinner. This was so very hard for me to believe. I started to pray, asking for his intercession. I would find myself talking to him. I wanted to find a priest like Padre Pio.

Shortly after reading the book, God revealed a sin to me. He showed me that by witholding my love from my husband, I disobeyed the greatest commandment of all, to love your neighbor. I could feel the pain in my heart. I had to get this one off of my chest. I went to confession. I waited for the priest to come in. Finally, I heard the door and I waited. I went back to the room and walked in.

It was an older priest that I had known from gradeschool. He did not even notice me when I walked in. I was so disappopinted, I walked back out in the Chapel where I talked with Jesus. I said to Him, "Jesus, I can not go to confession to him. The last time I went to him and confessed that I had a problem with forgiveness, he said to me, "That is ok. Jesus I need to have a different priest." After I was done complaining He told me to go back in there. I obeyed Him, and started with my confession. As I started to tell him and make excuses for my lack of love, he stopped me dead in my tracks. He said to me, "You are not here to talk about your husband. What were you like during those years?" I tried to come up with various excuses. They would not work. He said the words that still make me shake in my shoes. He said, "You need to come back in two weeks and think about what you have done." I sat there speechless, and the worst part was that he did not absolve me.

I walked out of the confessional not sure of what happened. I just knew this was not the same priest I remembered all of those years ago. The priest I knew was the fastest at saying Mass.

Jesus taught me a lesson that I will never forget. I was to never, ever, to talk about one of His annointed ones. He showed me that He loved all of His shepherds. He also gave me one of my wishes. I was able to go a priest that was just like St. Pio. Because of the fact I had a judgemental attitude, I was not given the gift of absolution.

The next time you are tempted to talk about a priest, be careful. I would recommend, you pray for them, instead of speaking about it. I did not even tell anyone but Jesus my complaint. He showed me that He did not appreciate it at all. Our beloved priests are humans. They are people with feelings. They have given up their lives to serve God, to be there to help us and guide us to Jesus. So pray for your priests and love them.

Make a decision to do something special for your parish priest. If each person who reads this actually does something nice for a priest, think of how many happy priests there would be. We always are there to take from them. We need to give back to them for once. Let us not think of ourselves but our priests.

I started to actively pursue my healing. I went to see Fr. Rookey several times, praying for healing, not just for me but also my family. God was doing something in my heart. He took me down this road slowly. I was on a journey. It was exciting and awesome. He took me to so many different places. He took me to places that I did not want to go. He also took me to places I never dreamt I would go. Life with God was not boring. It was the opposite, it was exciting and fun.

I found out, I could have fun without drinking. I could laugh with new friends God had brought into my life. We were having a good time. The best part was, we were all sober. We did not have to play games with each other. We all had many things in common. We had burdens and knew that God was the only answer. We were different in many ways, but we were all the same.

God had taken me where I needed to go this whole time. He was getting ready to ask me to go a little deeper, to trust Him and follow in His footsteps. Jesus was asking me to forgive. At this point I was sure I had forgiven all who had offended me. I had to admit that I still had some issues, but I thought I was done with forgiveness.

I had been working on this for a long time. He was asking me to forgive the people who had wounded me the most. I was not prepared for the pain I would need to go through in order to forgive. The good thing was that Jesus was there with me the entire time. He stayed close to me and held me in His arms. I was willing and He was able.

6

Love your enemies, and pray for those who persecute you, so that you may become the sons of your father in heaven. (Matthew 5:44)

Forgiveness

Jesus did not say hold bitterness in your heart for your enemies. He said love your enemies, which is very difficult. For us it may be, but with Jesus all things are possible. At times, only Jesus can assist us in the forgiveness process.

He is the perfect example. While He walked on this earth, He taught us what it means to forgive. You can find many scriputres that show us what we are to do. Even at the end after they beat him, were killing him, did he not say, "Father, forgive them, they know not what they do"? How can this be? Who among us could forgive as Jesus did?

His words are His words. Although we may find it difficult to live by His example. He did not give us exceptions on whom we could forgive. It is what it is. Jesus did not tell us that it was okay if you hold resentment in your heart for those who hurt you. Why do you think many rejected him? They refused to follow him. It was, and still is, extremely difficult.

In this chapter, I will attempt to share with you my journey with Jesus on forgiveness. It has been a long journey that began 11 years ago.

When I was reading about forgiveness for the first time, and I was taken aback I just sat there and shook my head. I thought "Yeah, right, that is impossible." I thought it was ridiculous, how could I forgive the two young men who raped me? I hurt people with my tongue, and it would not faze me. I felt that it was better to hurt than be hurt.

This worked for me; it kept people afraid of me. I had a reputation that I liked. You did not mess with Rocky.

It was then that I heard this small voice bringing up that word again forgive. I finally was desperate enough to try it. I started making a list of those I needed to forgive. Every day I would read the names and pray that God would help me to forgive them. I started to feel some relief. My list kept growing day by day. Jesus was very gentle with me.

I was not raised hearing about forgiveness or the importance of it. It went against everthing that I had ever believed. I used to say "I don't get mad, I get even."

During that time in my life, I was miserable. I was full of hatred. I hated the men who raped, the people who molested me, Bill, and my dad for dying. All you would have to do was look at my face and see the anger.

If the pain is left in your heart and no forgiveness has taken place, our hearts become hardened. We will put up walls to keep others out. The only problem is that the walls also keep God out. Without God's love in our hearts, we can never be healed.

What is in our hearts will come out of our mouths. It affects how we speak and talk to others. Unforgiveness affects a person in all areas of life. If we choose to hold on to the poison, it will kill us.

Although I started to want to forgive, I found it so difficult. I didn't feel that I was making any progress in this area. I always had someone that I needed to forgive.

I started to see people whom I needed to forgive. This was difficult for me. I would feel different when I was around them. He started to show different events that caused me pain. They were all on the surface. Inside I was trying to forgive, but my emotions did not cooperate. I would start to act crazy.

I began to see I needed to forgive the two young men who raped me. I began to pray for them. I had learned that if you hold onto the unforgiveness, you will be a prisoner of the event forever, that it will continue to hurt you over and over again. If you will not let it go, God can not come in and heal that wound. I was starting to get it. I wanted to feel better more than I wanted to hold on to the pain.

I talked with Jesus about my struggles. At Mass I studied the crucifix. As I looked at Jesus I was amazed. After all we had done to him, and how they beat Him to death, Jesus still forgave. I prayed, "Jesus, I can not do it. I do not know how you did it. I need your help; I can not do it without you." I went to Communion and went home. I did not think anything more about it.

That night I had the most beautiful dream. I was a green field. I saw an altar made of stones. There was a man standing behind it. I knew that he was a holy man. He had the most beautiful eyes. Although we did not speak, I could hear him talking to me. I could feel love coming from his eyes.

He held up one finger and said, "You see this finger, all I have to do is touch your head once and it will be done." He touched my head and I was consumed with peace.

When I woke up in the morning I still felt the same way. Something changed for me that day. My heart was becoming softer. I had a much easier time forgiving.

Sometimes I would make a little progress, and then I would fall again. Every time that I went to confession I had to confess some new unforgiveness that popped up. I needed a little more help. But I was determined to work on this. I was not going to give up.

I attended my first conference. It was to be held in Chicago. I had never experienced anything like that before. There were 1000 people, plus. All were there to pray and learn more about our faith. I was broken and full of anxiety.

I was trying so hard to follow Christ. It was so difficult for me. I was willing to do anything I could to cooperate with Him. Jesus knows His sheep and how to handle them. In the beginning, He carried me and I thank Him for that. If not, I surely would have died.

My heart was touched at this retreat. I could feel the presence of Our Lady. She was so near to me almost hugging me and wiping my tears.

It was an amazing experience, a weekend of prayer. I did not think I could pray that long. It was at this retreat that I heard Fr. DeGrandis speak. I was introduced to the Holy Spirit this weekend. I was not very familiar with the Third person of the Trinity. This was all new to me. Father spoke about the importance of forgiveness. I was not sure if it was possible, but I was willing to ask for it. I knew that I still had major issues with unforgiveness. I purchased a book of his, *Forgiveness and Inner Healing*.

We all prayed the Forgiveness Prayer together. We then prayed for each other for healing. The tears started flowing and I could not control them. I was sobbing uncontrollably. It felt good to get all of the tears out. I had kept them in for so very long. God had sent me help that weekend.

Fr. DeGrandis told us to say the Forgiveness Prayer every day for 30 days. If we did that something wonderful would happen. The weekend was the beginning of a wonderful journey with Jesus. The little book was a guide that assisted me on this journey.

I had my good days and my bad days. But I kept on. I noticed the phrase in the Lord's Prayer, "Forgive us our trespasses, as we forgive those who have trespassed against us." That terrified me; I was asking God to forgive me as I forgave others. I knew that I needed Him to forgive me from my past. So this was another motivator for me.

After praying the forgiveness prayer for thirty days, something beautiful happened. I was sitting outside enjoying a beautiful summer day. I was looking at the trees in my yard. All at once I was back at the woods where the rape took place. I was on the ground and just when I was going to be raped, Jesus walked out of the woods. The two young men looked at Him, and started weeping. Jesus opened His arms and they ran to Him. He hugged them; I could see that He loved them. I was a bit confused, I thought, "They were going to hurt me. Why would He go to them first?"

Jesus came to me and was starting hugging me. Tears were streaming down my face. I heard Him speak to me. He said "Raquel, these two young men are a mess because of what they did to you. You are the only one who can help them. Will you do that for me?" I looked at Him. I loved Jesus more than I hated them. So I agreed, I would pray for their healing. I started to pray for their lives to be whole.

I decided to make a pilgrimage to Chicago to stand in for these two young men. I attended a healing service that Fr. Peter Mary Rookey was holding at Our Lady of Sorrows in Chicago. I dedicated the day to praying for my abusers. Once I was able to pray for these men, I was given the grace to forgive. Jesus loves all of us. Even those people who have hurt us. His love for them is no different than His love is for us.

He never gave up on me, so I am not to give up on others. This is the hardest thing at times. Sometimes people do not act very nice. It is difficult to love the unlovable. I was like St. Mary Magadeline when I came to Jesus. Jesus loved her very dearly. She was special to Him. So I have to believe that I am as well.

Jesus' whole life was love. What He did was for each and every one of us he did out of love. Jesus loved the tax collectors and the prostitutes. He had a special place in His heart for what the world would call "low". He came for the sick. He is still in the business of healing, He can and will set us free. The only thing we have to do is let Him in.

At times we are in denail. We stuff the anger deep down in our hearts. We will do whatever it takes to avoid looking at painful memories. Pretending all is well with us, and nothing is wrong.

I had such a difficult time admitting that I was angry with my dad. How could I be mad at him? He was dead; he could not even defend himself.

I would just pretend that I was not mad at him. The problem was that I would find myself blaming him for the terrible things that happened to me. He was not even around; he had been dead for so many years. How could he be the problem?

When I finally was able to admit that I was mad at him. I began to heal. I was very confused. I had held him on this pedestal for so long. He could do no wrong. I had to look at the truth. I would scream at him, and tell him exactly what I thought about everything. I wanted to forgive him, but did not know how to. I could not understand being so mad at someone, and at the same time loving him.

This was the most difficult thing I had done up to this point. That meant I had to go back and visit the painful memories of the past. I tried to run from all of the ugliness, shame and times of uncertainty. It was so hard. As children we looked up to our parents. I know that I thought my parents could do no wrong. They took care of me, and fed me.

How we are raised greatly impacts our adult life. If we are raised with insecure parents, we will be insecure. Everything that our parents did will affect us. We are under their control. I do not know if parents realize how much they affect children. If you are raised in a particular enviroment, you can bet that it will seem normal as adults. If your parents drink, the children will most likely grow up to drink.

If the parents are not doing the right things, children will probably grow up to do the same things. We all are taught by example; we think and act like our parents. This was difficult for me. My parents argued when I was growing up. I thought it was normal, so I fought like they did. My dad had a bad temper and so did I.

I carried the anger in my heart for so many years. Once I let it out, and started to face each painful memory, it did not have the hold on me that it once had. I had to give it to God. The more I was able to do this, the more peace I felt. I was actually able to come to a point where I wanted to forgive my dad.

I spent many hours in prayer. I spoke to the priests in confession about this problem. I felt like I was stuck. It seemed that after all of the prayers and confession, I still was angry at him. I talked to God about this problem, over and over again. I gave God my free will, and told the Father that I desired to forgive my dad. I did not know what else to do.

I received many graces after communion. The tears would come and I could not control them. I asked for His help and He was coming to me during this special time.

I can not exactly remember the moment, but I have forgiven my dad. I am not mad at him anymore. Today I love my dad. I now know that both he and my mother did the best that they could.

My dad was trying to be a parent the best way he knew how. I can remember during the difficult times when I was angry with my dad. My mom told me "Raquel, your dad loved you kids more than anything else in the world. Everything that he did, he did for you kids. He did the very best he could." I now believe it with my whole heart.

If we deny our feelings and events that have happened in the past, we will never be whole. We will always be held captive. I know that it is okay to angry with someone, just remember to not let the sun go down on your anger. If you do not deal with it, it will become unforgiveness.

The hardest person to forgive was me. I was very hard on myself. I did not need anyone to beat me up; I could take care of it on my own. I could not look in the mirror without finding ten things wrong with me. I had a hard time looking at my past.

When I came back to the church, I wanted to forget all about that old girl. I wanted to be a different person. Although I loved Jesus, there was still so much of the old behavior left in me. I carried so much guilt and shame. I had shame for the things done to me, and what I did to others.

I was angry at myself for the mistakes I had made. How could I forgive myself when I did not like me? I had to believe I was forgiven. I went to confession and received absolution, my sins were forgiven. I would continue to confess the same sins over and over again. I could not accept the gift of forgiveness.

After I came back to the church, I had this idea that I would be a different person. I would be normal and have the perfect family. All I would need to do was to pray. While these things are true, we do have to participate in the process.

My heart hurt because I offended God. Jesus was becoming so real to me, a friend that I hurt by my actions. This motivated me to continue to take a look at my actions and my past. Today it continues to motivate me to go to confession at least once a month. If He was willing to stand by my side during the darkest hour of my life, that is the least I could for Him.

Although I had been working on forgiveness for some time. I still had this emptiness in my heart. My heart was still so wounded from my past. I did not know what to do. I knew the problem was in my heart. I wanted to feel better. I felt as if part of me was missing. One day in adoration I prayed, "Jesus, I need your help. I do not know what is wrong with me. Jesus, I just want to be whole." With that, I left the chapel unsure if He heard me.

7

The Lord is near the brokenhearted, and saves the crushed in spirit.
(Psalm 34:18)

I want to be whole

About two weeks after my request in the Adoration chapel, I had received a phone call from a friend of mine. She called to let me know that Fr. Sudac would be in the Chicago area for a two-day retreat. Fr. Sudac is a Catholic priest from Croatia. We decided to make the small pilgrimage to see this priest who we heard about.

It was an intense retreat that changed my life. When I heard Father speak, I knew that he was the one God was going to use to help me. I had no idea how but I was certain that I would be healed. Father Sudac was very humble. He wanted no attention to be on him, only on Jesus. He spoke of things that are so simple yet so deep.

He spoke of love and forgiveness. Father also talked about surrender. At this point, I had been trying to change myself and still be in control. I had no idea on how I could ever surrender all to Jesus. The weekend brought more blessings than I expected. Little did I know this weekend would be the answer to many prayers.

The last day of the retreat, people were handing out flyers which I read when I got to my seat. It was an invitation to attend a retreat in Mali Losinji with Fr. Sudac for five days. The best part of it was that we would also be spending six days in Medjugorje. I felt this wave of excitement rush through me.

I smelled roses. I tried to dismiss it as someone's perfume. I asked a few of my friends who were sitting next to me if they smelled the roses. They did not seem to smell the strong aroma of flowers. I turned to the left and asked my friend on the other side of me. She looked at me almost thankful that I smelled the roses and said with a big smile, "Yes I do."

I looked down at the flyer I held in my hand and said, "Our Lady, do you want me to go?" I could still smell the roses. I shook my head and said to her, "Well, if you want me to go you will need to talk to Steve about this." Never in a million years did I believe he would agree to it. I dismissed the idea as crazy and forgot all about the roses.

I surrendered my life to Christ at this retreat. It was extremely emotional for me. I could feel something different to my heart. With eight words "I surrender my life to you, Jesus Christ" my life and destiny were forever changed.

I did not understand the full impact of this at the time. I knew it was big; however I did not realize just how big it was. I did not know that it meant my family, job, the way I spoke to others, the way I dressed, even my thoughts. All of that had to be changed. The last thing that I expected from this was a healing.

When I returned home I expected to see miracles happening all over the place. I woke up before everyone else did, and prayed. I thanked Jesus for what He had done over the weekend.

My husband had returned from early morning Mass and I heard a gentle voice in my heart. It said, "Ask your husband about Medjugorje." I was so surprised at this I could not believe my ears. I said, "I just returned from a weekend trip. How can I ask him to leave for thirteen days?" Again I heard, "Just ask him." I asked him and he said yes. I thought I was hearing things. He said I could go if the money showed up.

As luck would have it, bonus time at work had arrived. This year the bonus had reached a record high. I had the money to go on my trip overseas. I guess I was going to Medjugorje and Mali Losinji. I called the pilgrimage director and told her that I would be sending my deposit. Not even a month had passed since I returned from the retreat and my trip was paid in full. I was going to Europe.

Preparation for the trip was crazy. The atmosphere was heating up at home. It seemed like all hell was breaking loose. I could not believe all of the things that were happening. Many times I thought I should just stay home and not go. Maybe things would be better if I cancelled the trip.

July the 23rd was here before I knew it. I had spent months preparing to go. It is amazing what kinds of thoughts went through my head. I was worried about the plane crashing. I would never forgive myself if I was on the other side of the world and a tragedy occurred.

I was sure of one thing; I would not come back to the United States the same girl who left. With all of that, I still made the decision for which I'll always be grateful. I went to Europe with five of my friends, to a small village that I had heard so much about.

My Daddy Never Died

The journey to Medjugorje took twenty-four hours. My luggage was lost and all I had was my carry-on case. The only good thing for me was that my cousin had brought extra clothes. We happened to be the same size.

Upon arriving at Medjugorje I was speechless. I could not believe I was actually there. We were shown to our room and we cleaned up for dinner. It was such a beautiful place, so peaceful and quiet. We introduced ourselves at dinner and the trip began.

Adoration would be taking place at St. James that evening at 9:00. The church was beautiful and full of people. It was moving for me. I could not help but think of the US and how Jesus is left alone in so many of the Adoration Chapels. Here in this little village, it was hard to fit all of the people in the church.

As I knelt down in the church, something happened. I felt a force coming entering my heart. It is hard to describe, I could feel small pressure entering into my heart. It lasted the entire time we were in Adoration.

This was the beginning of such a special trip. It was such a time of Grace for me. God had to take me to the other side of the world, to get me alone so He could do with me what He needed.

We attended daily Mass, prayed the rosary, went to confession and heard several of the visionaries speak. It was such a time of peace and solitude. One day at Mass, I asked Jesus to allow me to feel His love for me. As I received Holy Communion, I could feel deep love in my heart. I was so overwhelmed, and tears would not stop coming. I felt the love of God. It was so gentle but strong, not overpowering yet intense. I now have felt this love over and over as He has healed me.

The trip was filled with many experiences that emulated the love God had for me. I was getting very comfortable in the little village. I knew my way around and the schedule at St. James. My heart was being prepared for the trip to Mali Losinji. My luggage still had not arrived. At this point I was beginning to worry. I spoke with the pilgrimage leader, asking what would happen if my luggage did not arrive before we left Medjugorje. She just looked at me and said, "You will not get until we reach the States." As I walked out on the patio and heard a small voice in my heart, "My apostles followed me with nothing but the clothes on their backs." It was a joke within the group; they would make fun of me for wearing the same clothes.

The last full day in Medjugorje arrived. We started preparing to journey to Mali Losinji. As I spoke with my roommate I opened her Bible. A small piece of paper fell to the ground. I picked it up and it had one word written on it, Antonio. That was the ticket; I forgot to ask St. Anthony to find the lost luggage. I said a small prayer and enjoyed the rest of the day.

It was not long before my luggage appeared in the lobby. To this day no one was aware how it got there. At dinner all of the group clapped, and commented on how great I looked. I was the only one who had clean clothes to wear. Guess who was laughing now. That's right, me.

The trip to Mali Losinji was also a twenty-four hour journey. We would travel by bus and a ferryboat on the Adriatic Sea. This would be an experience that I would never forget. How in the world did I deserve to be here? I thank God that my husband always sticks to his promises. When long ago he promised I could go to Medjugorje.

The ferryboat was nothing like a cruise ship that I thought it would be. The rooms were very small. You either had a bathroom or air conditioning. We happened to be on the side of the boat with the air conditioning. For me this was not too great. I was always worrying about my hair. I never went very far without my hairspray.

We all met in the dining room for dinner. By this time the sun was setting. It was beautiful, being out on the ocean in the dark. The only light was the moon, which seemed to be so very bright. I only wished that Steve were there with me. He was on the other side of the world. Hopefully he was thinking about me.

We stayed at the Hotel Aurora, which was on the Adriadic Sea. It was more like the rest of the world. I went to the beach to unwind and gather my thoughts for the evening.

I thought back to the retreat in Chicago, five months ago. I could not imagine what the next five days would be like. God had heard all of my prayers. It was Our Lady who invited me and took care of all of the arrangements. For this I am forever grateful.

The retreat was held at the Bethany House. We met in a small room on the second floor. It reminded me of the upper room where the apostles waited for the Holy Spirit. There were about 50 of us, from every walk of life. But in this little room we were all the same. All of us were here searching for something. In need of something, we all held deep within our hearts. Father came in and we introduced ourselves. I was very nervous, I felt very vulnerable.

For the next six days we would all be together from 8 in the morning until 10 in the evening. I learned that many of us had pains in our hearts. Much to my surprise, many of my fellow pilgrims had problems far worse than mine.

The next six days were full of grace and much needed healing. The day would begin with spiritual talks and then we would have lunch at the retreat house. We had about three hours each day to relax. During the week, we received several blessings and prayers for healing. It was such an emotional time for me. I prayed to be healed from the rape and the death of my dad. I had been controlled by those events for as long as I could remember. I was ready to get rid of them once and for all.

I could not wait to return to my new life that I was sure awaited me. My family would all be changed. I was ready for this, I had been praying for about three years for all of this to happen. That is why I came on this trip; I wanted my family to be perfect and live happily ever after.

The days seemed to pass very quickly. This was the first time in my life that I was myself, with almost no masks. I could just sit and be me. I did not have to be a mom, wife or an employee. I could just be a child of God not having to perform, just me. I let it all out for the first time in 33 years; I could not hold back all of the tears. They would keep coming, one after the other.

My heart had been touched in a way that it had never before. I had no control of this; God came in with such a force that I have never been the same. I had to decide to let God in. Either I opened my heart to God or I would continue to remain a prisoner forever. I had finally gotten to the point in my life that I was sick of what I was doing. I was sick of being angry and full of pain. This trip gave me hope for a better life and that I could be different. I did not want to die feeling this way. Living the rest of my life the way I had was not an option at this point.

The only problem was I thought that my healing would be immediate. I expected to come home to all new things. I thought that I would never think about the rape or the death of my dad. I was sure that I would be this brand new person.

I had already felt better. I did not expect to get any resistance when I came back. I was expecting my family to greet me with open arms. Father had warned us that we had been changed, but those around us might not have changed. I ignored that comment, I was sure he was not talking about my family. He had told us to let the seeds that God had planted take root.

Until now, I did not understand what he meant. I believe that I am still receiving powerful healings from my trip.

The day came when we would be returning home. I did not want this to end. I wished that it could last forever. We attended Mass for the last time at Bethany house. It was very sad. We had all become like a family over the last two weeks. We arrived as strangers and left there as a new family.

Father asked each one of us to take the love God had given us, and share it with our families. Many tears were shed; it was hard to say good-bye. Father Sudac, like many of our beloved priests, sacrificed his time and was there to help God's people. He was there to teach us, and most of all, to show each of us the love God has for his children.

The plane ride home was very different for me. I could not speak. All I knew was that something had changed for me over there. I knew one thing for sure: I was not the same. Somehow I knew that I was getting ready to go into the battle zone. I did not know what was waiting for me, but I knew it was going to be the most difficult time of my life.

8

Be strong in the Lord and in His power. Put on the whole armor of God, so that you may be able to stand against the wiles of the devil. (Ephesians 5:10-11)

The Fight

When the flight finally landed at O'Hare, I was exhausted. I was very anxious to see my family. I could not believe that it had been two weeks.

We had to pass through customs, which it was nothing like you see in the movies. I did not see anyone being led away for questioning, or anything exciting. The agent just looked at my passport and said, "Have a good day Ms. Hanic." That was all there was to it. I was back in the good old USA.

For the second time on this journey, my luggage was lost. Apparently it did not make the flight. We were told it was still in Croatia. Things are a bit different in the States. The airlines actually knew where my luggage was. They were even going to deliver it to me at home. The only thing that I was worried about was all of the rosaries that I brought back from Medjugorje. I was certain that Our Lady would see that they would get home safely. Many people were in need of the little beads that contained so much grace.

Before picking up the children, I made my first stop at the Adoration Chapel. I gave thanks to Jesus. He had been there for me so much. I would be visiting Him many more times over the next the years. I went back to work the day after I returned home. Things had to get back to normal, or so I thought.

The first few days were great. I felt as if I were on top of the world. I had so much peace it was unbelievable. Then, all at once, things took a dramatic turn.

My oldest daughter started to have many problems. It first started at school, and then it was her being late. She was thirteen at the time. My daughter and husband started fighting. It was awful; I could sense evil creeping into our house.

The pressures at work seemed to increase and I was being pulled in a hundred directions. I thought, "This will not last long, I am just suffering from jet lag."

To top it all off, I started having flashbacks. At first I thought I was going crazy. I knew something had been shaken overseas. All of the junk was coming up so fast I could not keep my breath.

As the weeks passed to months, conditions at home and work got worse. I was starting to get very confused, not to mention angry for the miracle not happening.

It was early one morning, while I was crying out to God, that I was led to a scripture. "When a unclean spirit has gone out of a person, it wanders through waterless regions looking for a resting place, but not finding any, it says 'I will return to my house from which I came.' When it comes, it finds it swept and put in order. Then it goes and brings seven other spirits more evil than itself, and they enter and live there; and the last state of that person is worse than the first." (Luke 24:24-26). When I read this I was terrified. What in the heck did He mean by this? Surely this was given to me for someone else. I also heard a voice telling me to read the book of Job. I have never heard about Job before.

After reading the book of Job, I was not a happy camper. I had been through enough in my short life. Surely, I was mistaken. Well I am here to tell you that I was not. I was about to enter a very dark and lonely period of time.

Apparently, God had figured that I could handle going through the healing process right along with all of this. I was just like the Israelites after they were freed from the Egyptians. They were wandering in the desert complaining, wishing they were back in bondage. It was terrible. There was no way that I was going to get through this alone.

I was spending every day during my lunch hour at the Adoration Chapel. I would sit and cry for hours. I had so much pain in my heart it was unbearable. I was very confused about my life and what God was doing.

I could not talk to anyone about this. I had such a hard time expressing what was happening on the inside of me. Through all of this I still had to go on as if nothing were happening. In reality, I wanted to explode from all the crap that was surfacing.

The scab had been torn off and I felt as though I was bleeding to death.

During this time I was not thanking God for what He was doing. I believed I was being punished for all of my past sins, the ways I had offended God and hurt others in my life.

I felt so many emotions during those 36 months. The flashbacks continued, almost as if I were watching a movie. It was during these painful memories I realized the numerous times that I was molested by various individuals.

I used to wonder why I could not remember a large part of my childhood. I had blocked them out. All humans have a built-in survival mechanism. When the trauma is too much, we will bury it, in hopes that it will go away. The only problem is that these events will affect our personalities and how we react to situations for the rest of our lives. We become prisoners of our past.

I have learned that unless we go back we cannot and will not receive healing. That is the most difficult thing for an abuse victim to do, go back. For many of us we have carried around so much shame from our past. We are embarrassed about the situation and are worried what people will think. We blame ourselves for the ugliness that happened to us. I blamed myself for the rape. That is what kept me from telling anyone. The violation was so great and the shame that went along with it was so deep. How could anyone understand me, and what I felt?

I had no faith in God. I knew Jesus, and, of course the Blessed Mother. But I did not know who God the Father was. I was afraid of Him and did not believe He could love me. I had always kept my distance from God, fearing the next punishment He would send my way.

All of this has changed. I now believe with all of my heart that the Father loves me, and I belong to Him. I am His child and He is my Father. I had heard many times that you had to receive His forgiveness and love in order to give it. I could not receive His love or His forgiveness. I did not feel that I was worthy of such Grace.

I started to talk to God, crying to Him about the past and how it hurt me. He would always lead me to scripture that would offer such hope for the suffering. I found myself talking to Him more and more. It was a beautiful thing that was happening. I do not even know when the moment came that I realized that The Father loves me but I thank Him for His patience with me. I did not trust anyone, and to be honest, that included God.

He led me to one scripture numerous times. "And you will know the truth, and the truth will make you free." (John 8:32) I was not going to be free until I looked at the past. This time my Daddy would be there with me wiping away all of the tears.

The enemy was attacking me. I do not want to give him too much credit so I will limit my writing. I endured some of the most bizarre and crazy assaults. At first I was terrified of them. I would always talk about them at great length. I wanted to get some sort of relief from the invasions. It did not come. God allowed me to go through them. It was all for my own good, to teach me, and He did. I did not like what I learned. I was giving the devil glory. I was giving him power over me. He was able to scare me and it worked. In my warped mind he was more powerful than God.

I believed all of my problems and circumstances were much bigger than God. How crazy is this type of thinking? This is the thinking of a broken little girl who saw much evil and pain for most of her life. I did not think that God would do any good, that He just stood by and let all of this happen to me. These were just a few of the many lies that I believed.

I had to endure years of this type of attacks before I finally caught on. The devil is a liar, and he is nothing in comparison to the Almighty who just happens to be my Father. When this finally hit me, it freed more than I can say. All things have to pass through the hands of God. When I am under the attack, I thank God. I may have opened a door that will need to be closed. God may be allowing me to go through it to be strengthened. But now I will give God the Glory instead of the devil. He deserves this from us. No matter what is happening, God will use it for good. He is in total control of my life, and He must have willed it. It must be good, because God is good.

God also taught me the importance of praise and worship. Being a Catholic all of my life, I was used to singing the same songs for years. I love those songs and they are beautiful. What I am talking about is praising and worshiping God, singing a love song to Him for all that He has done. I include this in my daily prayers to my Daddy.

He led me to the Old Testament, where God's people were under attack. His instructions to them were to praise Him. That sounds very crazy. To praise God when you are ready to be ambushed. They would have to take their minds off of themselves and their problems. They would need to focus on God and praise Him. I thought to myself, "They must have been crazy. If I were there, I would be ready to fight." I continued to read on. The amazing thing that happened was the enemy was so confused they slaughtered themselves.

Take a moment and think about this. When we focus on God, and not the bigness of the problem, He can move. We are actually displaying faith, not in us, but in the God who cares. The same God who sent Moses to free His people. If we had faith that He loves and cares about us, we would believe He will heal us.

Praise and worship are a beautiful thing and a powerful weapon while under attack. This cannot and should not take the place of prayer. I still pray the Rosary, Divine Mercy, and read the Bible. I attend Mass as often as I can. I read the Bible and focus on God's promises.

I experienced so many healings in my heart when I received Jesus in Holy Communion. You must believe that He is truly present in Holy Communion. Read the Bible if you have a hard time with this one. At the Last Supper, He instructed the apostles. He broke the bread and said "Do this in memory of me. This is my body, given up for you." This is a truth that the Holy Spirit can bring into your heart.

After receiving Holy Communion I would ask Jesus for healing. It could be with unforgiveness, fear, and pains from the past. He always answered my request and healed my heart from the many burdens that I had carried for so long. Jesus is present in the Holy Eucharist, and is more than capable of healing you. The only thing that is required of you is that you open your heart and believe.

It took me such a long time to see the good that God had been doing in my life, for me to even see that He was answering my prayers. My entire family was going through a major healing. I was not very patient with Him and His timing. I wanted what I wanted. I was spoiled and used to getting things my way. Well, God was not going to have any part of that old behavior.

I was fighting God and it would be a fight that I could never win. There are still many times that I attempt to fight God. I wish that I did not, but honestly I do. The difference is that I give up a lot sooner now.

I spent so much time blaming the devil and those around me for the uncomfortable times that I was going through. God knows each of His children and what it will take to get us where we need to be. He is very patient and kind in the process. Most of the time He is answering our prayers, but it can be hard to see at the time. We can become frustrated with the process.

It is very difficult to put on paper all of the healings He has given. I had to pay a price for each and every one. I had to do many things that I did not want to do. I had to become vulnerable and open myself up. I had to be obedient to Him or I would not have the healings. Many of the things that I had to do were to humble myself; I did not like this very much. I had always elevated myself due to my low self-esteem. I had to lower myself and admit my faults.

I was afraid of being rejected. I could not take another pain in my heart. I had to expose myself to the ones who were the closest to me. I had convinced them I was strong, and that I did not need anyone. The truth is, I craved their love and needed them so much. I had such a hard time expressing myself.

I can talk with the best of them, just not about the things that I needed. I could talk about everything else but the truth that was in me. I would always guard myself to protect that little girl.

I had to take the step of faith that God was true to His word and He would do what He said He would. So far, He has not let me down. He has worked on breaking down the walls that were surrounding my heart.

I have kept a fort around my heart with many armed guards, like anger, coldness and the pretense that I was so strong. I could fool the best of them, not God though. He knew the real me. I was very sensitive and would get wounded easily. Actually, I expected to be hurt.

God knew all of my past and the wounds that were deep in my heart, so with enabling grace, He was very gentle with me. He never asked me to do something that I could not do. I still had the choice. If I did what He asked, I would get freedom, but if I chose to run, I would remain stuck in Fort Rocky.

I started to come out little by little. I did still get hurt, but this time I understood. I would react from that wounded part of me. It was a sign for me that I was still in need of healing.

God began to show me how I could protect myself from getting hurt. I could not say the things that were deep in my heart. I would pretend that situations did not bother me. In all honesty, I was dying inside. I would overreact to situations because my feelings were hurt.

I could not take any correction. I perceived it as rejection. I would become very defensive and be easily offended. I was very hard to get along with; everything was about me.

I had a problem with anger. I could fly off the handle in less than 60 seconds. At work, my nickname was Chili Pepper. The name fit me well.

I have to be honest: I liked it. If I could convince people that I was crazy, they would not mess with me. I did a good job in this area.

My personality was warped from all of the pain. I did many things to keep from feeling pain like I did as a child. The problem was that I was hurting others and had made so many wrong choices. The choices caused me so many problems. I hurt people because I had been hurt. When God started to take me down this road, I was very sad. This time, it was because of all of the hurt I caused.

I did not want to look at all I did. My life was no longer my own. I did not like where I was heading. He was preparing me to live the life of surrender. A life I had believed was for the weak. I wanted to be strong at all costs, so this was not easy for me. Surrender to me meant that I would be giving up. God used this time to teach me true strength that comes from surrender.

9

So, I will boast all the more gladly of my weaknesses, so that the power of Christ may dwell in me....for when I am weak, then I am strong. (2 Cor. 12:9-10)

Surrender

I don't know about you, but I had many different thoughts on surrender. I mean the surrender that many of the saints speak of, not what most of us had been taught.

God began to invite me to surrender all to Him. I say invite because we do have free will and it is up to each one of us to say yes or no.

Surrender to me was to give up and quit fighting. This is not something that ROCKY did. She was a fighter. To me surrender meant that you lost. The only thing left to do was to give up.

To me that was a sign of weakness. You have to take care of yourself or no one else would, right? My dad used to tell me, second best is never good enough.

So when I was being taught about surrender I thought people must be crazy. It went against everything that I ever believed. I would do whatever it took to win, to survive.

I had to be in control. I was the one who had to make things happen, a shaker and a mover. I was an adult and finally in control of what happened in my life.

I was also going to be the one to fix everyone else, my husband, children, brothers and sisters. The inside of my heart was a mess but I was thinking that I could fix others. If you looked at other people then you would not have to look at yourself. I pretended I was all together. Because if I looked too closely, I might just fall apart.

A Christian friend had a sign on her desk. She would look at it each morning. In big bold letters was one word, "SURRENDER." I remember reading the sign on her desk thinking, "Poor girl she just sits there and lets things happen in her life." It appeared to me that she was doing nothing. I could not even begin to understand this way of thinking. I thought that she was crazy.

Well not me. If you want something badly enough you've got to make it happen. That is exactly what I did, and God allowed me to think that it was all me. He let me run until I finally wore myself out. I was exhausted, angry and full of anxiety. At this point in my life my prayers were specific and exact requests.

My prayers were to control, manipulate and change those around me. Prayers to make those that I was around easier to live with, selfish, self-centered, prayers all about me. They were requests to make me feel better about my life so that I could be happy.

The funny thing, is that they did not get answered the way that I thought. God always answered the prayers when I was praying for His Will. If I would ask Him to speak through me, He would. He was slowly teaching me about surrender.

He did not answer the specific demands that I called prayers. The more that I prayed the more He began to show me that I was the one that needed to be changed. What a concept, that there could be anything wrong with me.

My Father began to show me how He was removing the things from my life that were no good for me, so that He could move in. Things like talking badly about people, trying to fit in, compromising my values to get ahead at work.

All this was easy in comparison to surrendering my family to God. Truly letting go and trusting the creator of the universe with my loved ones. I was desperately afraid that if I let go and gave them to God that I would lose them.

In the end God won and I lost. I surrendered all to Him. My life, my family, my job, my pain, my childhood, and my past. All of the things I had held very near and dear to my heart.

I thank God that I was never alone for one moment. He promises, " I will never leave you or forsake you." He lived up to that promise. Up to this exact moment, He has never left me or forsaken me.

God began gently to show me I was controlling. I was holding on to so many people in my heart. My biggest issue was fear. I had fear of abandonment, fear of rejection, fear that they may even die.

He had shown me my controlling was hindering them. I was getting in His way. I thought I could change people and places. In a way I was trying to be God. I was holding on so tight, I was suffocating them. I was doing

Surrender

all of these things in the name of love.

The old saying is so very true. " If you love someone you have to set him free".

I have learned that is doesn't necessarily mean that they will leave or you will even lose them. But it does mean that you love them enough to let them be free to be themselves, free to make their own choices, and even to make mistakes. They also know that no matter what, you will love them in spite of it all. There are no conditions to real love. We are all human and make plenty of mistakes. We are not put here to withhold love from anyone. The problem is that so many of us do. We do not love as Jesus did.

When we love with no conditions, our loved ones will feel this acceptance. They will then feel free to be who God wants them to be. God is a very capable Father.

For so many years I would pray when I was in trouble or when someone in my family was sick. I had God on a shelf and I would pull Him out when I needed something. Forget me ever listening to Him. If He needed me to do something for Him, that was not even an option.

I started praying for God's will in my life. That was very scary for me. I wanted what He wanted. I wanted the job that He wanted me to have. Considering I had not done a great job, I could use a little help.

Needless to say He kept me out of many traps. I did not understand it then, but now I can clearly see. Now I include God in every decision I make. If it is His will let it be, but if not then let it pass. This type of prayer keeps me out of many terrible situations.

I believe many of us have fear of God and not the reverential fear. The fear that I now have is that I would hurt the one who loves me like God does. He has laws and commandments for a reason. If I choose to break a commandment then I will suffer the consequences. This is a healthy fear.

God had made me face each and every fear that was in my heart. You see, there were so many that had controlled me. It was extremely difficult. It was hard to see what all of the fears were. If I did not face the fears, I would continue to be controlled by the devil. He could and would continue to manipulate me like a puppet. This had happened for too many years.

The fears were bigger than God the Almighty was. God had to become bigger in my life than all of the pain. When we are stuck in the past, pains actually take on a life of their own. They are bigger than anything or anyone, including God.

It was not until I faced each fear, and surrendered them to God, gave them to Him as a gift, that the fears left. It was not something that happened over night. It took time and patience. I needed to recognize when I reacted out of fear, which was many times.

The fears would not leave without a fight. They were very comfortable in their cozy little homes. The only problem was that this house now belonged to God and His Most Holy Spirit. Someone had to go and it was not going to be God.

The war had begun and it was painful. The inside of me was bloody and exhausted. People could not see what was going in my heart. I did not think that I was going to make it out alive. I was certain that at any given moment I would need to be committed. God was now my Daddy and I was in the middle of His hand. He was carrying me through this difficult time. If it were not for Him I would have surely died.

I wanted to run very far away from all of this. It was like everything was crashing in on me. The only problem is wherever I ran, I took me along. I could not hide for one moment.

I thought when I surrendered my life to Christ that He was going to take it all away with His miracle working hands. All of the pains, problems, and people who were difficult for me to deal with would suddenly dissappear. I mean I was holy, now things should be going much easier for me. Boy, was I wrong.

Not only did my problems remain but they appeared to growing in large numbers. This is not what I had signed up for. I thought that I signed up for peace, and happiness. The perfect life with the perfect family.

When I returned from Medjugorje, I was sitting at the edge of my bed late one night. I was very distraught and confused about many things. I started talking to God. I was in so much pain and all I could say to Him was. "God, this is so hard." I heard Him speaking to me in my heart. He said, " Yes it is, Raquel. You say that you love my Son. But do you still love Him when things are difficult?" I could see each and every bad thing that had happened to me. The molestation, rape, all of the pains of my life. He then asked me a question. " Do you know why all of these things happened to you?" I replied, " No Lord I do not." He then said. " For my glory and honor." That was all that He needed to say

God began to show me that I had a bad attitude. I was negative and expected bad things to happen to me and my family. My mind needed to be renewed. I gave my mind to God and He had permission to do as He wished.

God would show me what to read, what to watch on TV and what not to do. My spirit could no longer watch anything that had violence in it. I read books on lives of the Saints and listened to many different teaching tapes. This helped me tremendously.

About a year had passed since the Surrender, I was making small baby steps, not giant leaps, just small steps of progress. There were some very real changes happening on the inside of me. They just had not made to the outside yet. That was still to come.

It was so difficult to talk about what was going on inside of me to my husband. I was having such a hard time understanding it, I could not imagine how he could. I was certain that he would think I was crazy if I told him everything. He was now living with a total stranger.

One day while I was in the Adoration Chapel. I had a vision of an old altar. I saw a man with young boy. I immediately knew that it was Abraham and Isaac. I could see it all, Abraham was placing Isaac on the altar and he was going to sacrifice him to God. Just before he could finish the angel came down and told him to stop. Abraham was then given a ram to offer as a sacrfice instead.

I can not even begin to imagine what was going on in Abraham's mind. God had given him Isaac as an answer to a prayer. He was a miracle child and then God asked him to give him back. What turmoil he must have endured while going up the mountain.

With this God revealed to me what true surrender means. Our loved ones belong to God. They are not ours. When we actually surrender them to God, we are trusting in Him, that He will take care of them. It is not our job to figure out their future. All we are to do is love them like God loves us. This was so difficult to do. I had so many fears that kept me from completely surrendering them to God. I had to work hard with God and pray for the grace to surrender. I had to let go and stop getting in God's way.

It does not mean that He will physically remove them. It does mean that He is in control of their lives.

So you see God has taught me that surrender is not for the weak. It is actually for the strong, for those whose faith is strong in the Father. "All things work for the good to those who love God." (Romans 8:28)

Surrender of your life and those that you love is the most beautiful gift we could give God. We give to Him all He has given to us. So then we can become what He intended. We can then fulfill the mission He has called us to.

Surrender for me is a day-by-day journey. I can always notice when I am holding on to something. I start to feel full of anxiety, and have lost my peace. It is then that I have to pray and ask God what I am holding on to. God is faithful and is always there to show me.

Today, surrender is not as difficult for me as it once was. I must admit that I am a work in progress. I still fight the need to be in control. I thank God that "His mercy endureth forever." I am constantly in need of this. I am weak, but He is strong.

To be a servant for Christ, surrender is a must. We can not say that we truly follow Him unless He is in control.

So today, make a decision and let Him lead you. You will not regret it. You can be certain that change will follow your decision. He will remove the things that keep you from Him. You will be a new creature in Christ. Invite Him into your heart, and let him show you who He intends you to be, what is His will for your life.

Remember He said, "Be not afraid, I go before you always. Come follow me, and I will give you rest."

10

Create in me a clean heart, O God, and put a right spirit in me. *(Ps 51:10)*

Purification

M y personality was warped from all of the pain. I did many things to keep from feeling pain like I did as a child. The problem was that I was hurting others and had made so many wrong choices. The choices caused me so many problems. I hurt people because I had been hurt. When God started to take me down this road, I was very sad. This time, it was because of all of the hurt I caused.

I did not want to look at all I did. I wanted to stay where I could look at what others did to me. I needed to look at all of these things. If not, I would still be hurting the ones I love. God was not going to tolerate it any longer.

God began to deal with me in all areas that needed to be cleaned up. Up to this point the focus was on all of the abuse that I endured. Now the winds had begun to change.

I already had a problem with low self-esteem, so to even look at bad qualities was very difficult. This time was the most difficult part of my journey. During this time I felt alone, that God had abandoned me. I had not felt peace in so long, just despair and darkness.

He would not let me get away with anything. I could not even raise my voice without feeling the Holy Spirit's conviction. I would get so mad, I felt like I was being dealt with on everything. I can clearly remember crying one day saying to God, "I am such a loser. Do I do anything right?" In my mind I would see a picture of my three-year-old daughter. That would be my clue that I was acting like a child.

He would take me back in time and show me situations how I acted. It was terrible, I was able to see all of the pain I had caused. It was so sick I could not stand it. I knew what it felt like to hurt, and I had been the one creating pain in so many people's lives.

I began to realize my selfishness. It was idolatry. This is another trick of the enemy to love self. I can see how easy it is because the hurts are very deep. We do have an obligation to work through this and allow God to come in to help us get rid of the things that are not of Him.

Up to this point I felt like I was a caring person. I have always had a big heart and thought that I cared about people. I quickly realized that most of the time I spent thinking about myself. I really did not have enough time left to think about anyone else but my problems.

I had prayed the prayers asking for healing, I wanted to change. I asked Jesus to take my heart and make it like His heart. I knew enough to know that my heart was not good. I would do things that I did not want to do. I had no control. I wanted to act differently, but it seemed that I had no self-control over many things.

To be honest, I did not even realize I was that far off. I thought that I was a good person who was caring. How wrong I was about so many things.

I was very hard and direct. I had no time to mess around. I can remember many conversations that I had, and I would say, "What is the bottom line?" I did not have time to hear any of the nonsense. I wanted the meat and the potatoes. I was not at all concerned with the small, unimportant details.

I am not a gentle person by nature. I have to work hard in the area of compassion. This is something that was very difficult for me. I was a very strong-willed person and my personality reflected this. I had a difficult time being kind and compassionate.

God also began to show me my motives. It was actually very sick when I started to see all of my motives, the reasons I said some of the things I did, why I behaved the way I did. I had so many hidden motives.

What drove me to do the things that I did not like about myself? If we take time to look at our actions, we will find an underlying motive. The truth needs to come out, so we can become people who have a pure heart and the right motives.

During this time I realized I had many masks. I would pull a different one out to fit the situation. I had myself convinced that if I said I was great enough times, eventually I would be. Well, needless to say it was all a big game to keep others away from me.

I did not even know the truth about me. How could anyone else? I had gotten very good at playing the game. I had the best job, the happiest family, and everything in my life was perfect. So as you can see, I was an expert in the area of denial. I could not and would not look at the truth. I had lived this big lie for so many years. I did not know how to be. I had to always be so strong. I had to be strong for my mom, my brothers and sisters, my husband and children.

I never allowed myself to be weak and vulnerable. I had to keep it all together; if not they would all fall apart. God even began to show me my motive behind all of the madness. I wanted to be superior, to be strong and to have the control.

He was breaking me down to show how weak I was. I did not like what I was seeing. I was an extremely negative individual, always expecting bad things to happen. I had even believed the lie, that I was positive. I would go over in my mind all of the bad things from my past.

During this time I attended many healing services asking for healing from each and every thing that God would bring up in me. I would go to Our Lady of Consolation, in Carey, Ohio, where we would be blessed with a first class relic of the True Cross. This was very powerful and healing for me. Our Lady was always willing to provide the consolation that she promised. She was there to love me and comfort me. She has been such a wonderful Mother to me.

I had to go through a time when I was mistreated by the ones that I love. This was a test to keep silent and to still love. In no way could I have done this without the help of the Holy Spirit. I had to pray almost minute by minute for self-control. To have a cover placed over my mouth, so that I would not say the things I wanted so say. I was required to forgive over and over again. I had to endure this for a year. This was such a painful time and I could not understand why I was being treated this way.

God allowed me to feel the way I had made others feel. I was rejected and I had rejected. I would wound with my mouth, and others wounded me with their mouth. I was judgmental and I was judged. It was terrible; I was being treated the way I had treated so many people in my life and I did not like it.

This time was such a blessing for me, to be on the other side. I can tell you that God says in His word, that He is a God of Justice. He allowed me to see just how it felt, to be mistreated. This reminded me to never ever do these things again. Today I can say I appreciate it, and will always remember this lesson.

During this time I was shown just how judgmental I have always been. I had thought I was better than other people. I had a problem, judging people who were heavy drinkers. It is hard to admit, but the truth. I had an extremely difficult time seeing this. I was an alcoholic at the age of fifteen but had not drunk in years. I was different now. I had no compassion for anyone who was drinking. I do not even know how I became this way.

When I finally quit drinking, I hated the drink and all it caused me. I hated bars and anything that reminded me of the old me. I had to stay away from those places, or else I would slip right back. So at the beginning I think that it was a good thing. It kept me from drinking. Then somehow it turned for the worse, I could not seem to separate the drink from the people.

The truth is that I hated that part of me. I had used alcohol for so many years to dull the pain. Since I had such a problem in this area, I figured so did everyone else. I could not picture anyone who was a social drinker.

God had tried to show me this for such a long time. I would not see it; I had hate in my heart. It was for me. I had to forgive myself for all of the things that I did when I was drinking. As I read the Bible I would be led to the scripture saying, "Why do you see the speck in your neighbor's eye, but do not notice the log in your own eye?" (Luke 6:41) For the longest time, I could not understand what this meant.

The word Pharisee comes to mind. During this time in my life, I was actively seeking God. I was going to church, and praying the Rosary. I was even praying for many people, and the problems they had in their lives. Yet I still had a judgmental attitude.

Pride was another major problem for me. I could not understand how someone who was rooted in rejection and lacked self esteem could have such a problem with pride? The combination did not seem to go together. But the truth was that I was full of pride.

It was confusing for me. For years I believed that pride was a good thing, to be proud of the accomplishments one has achieved. My dad used to tell me, "Raquel, always be proud of who you are." He went on to say, "Never be ashamed of being Mexican." As a child, I missed the message my dad was attempting to convey. He was trying to tell me not to let my heritage hold me back. I could accomplish anything that I set out to do.

When I returned to the church, I started to feel good about myself. Things started to change in me and I could actually see the sun shine again. I fell for a major trap; I was starting to take the credit for what God was doing in me. I had cooperated with God to do my part, but God had the hard job.

I wanted to feel good about myself, that I was willing to take the credit for what God had been doing. With this type of attitude, God was not getting the glory He so much deserved. Self always wants the credit, to be patted on the back, and receive the "atta boy." To hear the words, "good job Raquel."

I wanted to be praised for each and every thing. I would do good things for my family, expecting a compliment. If I cooked a great meal, I expected to hear, "That was delicious, thanks, mom."

There is nothing wrong with wanting your family to thank you for what you do. The problem for me was I needed to have these things to keep me going. I needed to be constantly told I was pretty or looked nice, to hear some compliment each and every day.

My family needed to keep me fixed. That was not fair on my part. If I am doing things for anyone, with a string attached, my motives are all off. If I cannot do something for people, just because I want to make them happy, then I have a major problem.

This was so hard for me to stop. I asked God to help me with this. He then started to answer my prayers. The compliments all stopped. I had to turn to God for the acceptance that I craved.

Running was something that I did most of my life. It did not take long before God started dealing with me concerning the ways I have attempted to run from my problems. Drinking was something that I did to run. I could see this pretty clearly. Work was another place I used to escape from the reality. There was a time in my life when I would have rather been at work than at home with my family.

It was during these years that my job became for me an escape. I was working as a supervisor at a Fortune 500 company. At work I had respect and felt as if I was accomplishing some goal.

My self-esteem was based on the job that I did. My jobs had always helped my ego. I was what the world would call successful. I was headed for promotions at this company. I wanted to make as much money as I could. I would then be somebody who had prestige and respect. I was addicted to drama and chaos. I lived liked that for so many years. I did not know any other way. Peace, to me, was extremely boring.

I was not at all used to having long period of peace. At first I loved it, the peace. I was tired and longed for the peace. It did not take me too long to become bored. I would create drama, a fight and then the peace was gone.

When God started to heal me, I felt a peace. I started to get bored and

My Daddy Never Died

went back to the old comfortable me, I am happy to say that I appreciate the peace of God and I long to keep it. Peace is a gift from God available for all of His children.

Many of the times our own choices cause the anxiety. We make decisions that will take the peace from us and we are back in the same boat as before. If we truly want the peace of God, we will need to make different choices and live the way He had instructed.

A major pain in my heart was my involvement in New Age. I went to a fortune-teller and bought an angel board. New Age spoke of peace and healing, which I longed for. I was very naïve. I did not know anything about what God had to say about all of this. The whole focus of New Age was self. Considering that I was full of myself I bought it hook, line and sinker.

I got what I deserved, more anxiety than I had before I began. I dabbled in this for a bit, until God called me back to the church where I was baptized. The Roman Catholic Church. He was there the whole time, waiting for my peace. His name was Jesus Christ of Nazareth. He is the way, the truth and the light.

I had opened a door, which was not going to be shut too easily. I had to be taught a lesson, I had to seek and learn what God had to say about this. What I discovered has brought me many tears. The decision I made held many serious consequences.

I realized that by my actions, I hurt God. He had been so gracious to me and loved me so many times. I had made decisions that caused my Father pain. He had to teach me a lesson like any good dad would.

I tried this thing with God and have not turned back since. It was been difficult and lonely at times. I will not lie and tell you that it was easy. The greatest thing for me is I can remember everything I did the night before. I can even remember the conversations I had. It is awesome. Somehow and somewhere along the way God has totally changed me. He was taken me and made something beautiful.

I finally was able to thank God for the struggles. I was being changed during this dark time in my life. How strange it was that I could thank him for the hardships. He said, " I will restore the years the locusts have eaten." (Joel 2:25)

The narrow road is difficult; doing the right things at times is difficult. Forgiving the ones who have hurt us is difficult. All of these things are not more difficult than living the wrong way. Living your life the wrong way,

Purification

making wrong choices over and over again, is painful. Doing the wrong things time and time again, and expecting something to change, is just crazy. It is not possible.

If you have had enough, and want to feel better, I am here to announce to you that your Father is waiting for you. His arms are wide open, and He is ready to touch your wounded heart. All you have to do is come to Him.

11

He said, "Come." So Peter got out of the boat, starting to walk on the water, and came towards Jesus. (Matthew 14:29)

The Call

People have always been drawn to me. I do not know if it is because I talk a lot or something else. I have never been accused of being a fake person. What you see is what you get.

I am a serious and passionate person, and do not like to play games. I am not a follower, but a leader. The problem with that is, before I came to the Lord, I would lead people the wrong way.

Everywhere I went people would open up to me. It was pretty normal for me. I know so many secrets about many people. I learned from my background to keep silent. It seemed that I always knew what to say, and what not to say.

I can not count the times I have heard from people, "I do not know why I am telling you this, but…" That was pretty normal for the conversations I had. I guess people felt safe with me. Even though I was far from the Lord, He was near to me. I have always had a big heart. I have so much compassion for others, and the pains they carry in their hearts. I would actually feel the pain of all the people I met. I would hurt for them and what they had gone through.

I have met so many women who were abused, rejected and abandoned. I have begun to think every person on this earth has suffered some sort of abuse. There are so many people with so much pain. What can be done about it?

I would meet with people and just listen. I had nothing else to offer them, only my ears and the compassion in my heart. If I let someone in my heart, I wanted to do whatever I could to help. At times this was overwhelming for me. What was I supposed to do with all of this junk? At this time I was still in a deep pit. My life was a mess; I was still trying to find peace.

When God called me back to the church and started the long journey of wholeness, each step that He had me take gave me so much relief. I wanted to share all of this with those I knew were suffering.

I began to see I was not the only one on my island. There were many people just like me.

Each person that I met and talked with shared one common thing. We all had this look in our eyes, a deep and dark pain that can only be seen through the eyes. I have heard that the eyes are the windows to the soul. If you ever go to talk with someone who had been abused, they can't look into your eyes. I was this way, afraid someone might be able to see the things that were deep in my heart.

God began to show me that He wanted me to open up. He wanted me to share my story with others. At first I would not listen, it was just too hard for me. While I was at Adoration with Jesus, I heard a small voice, "Wouldn't you share your story if one soul would be saved?" I answered back, "Yes, of course I would."

Little by little I began to open up. It was not as difficult as I thought. I actually felt some relief. As I would share, they would also share with me. Victims know that they are safe with other victims. We do not judge each other. We are all so hungry for some sort of acceptance and help. Victims feel that there is no help or hope for them. For most of us, that is what life had dealt us for so many years.

Some of the stories I heard made my life look like a piece of cake. So many out there have suffered so much. I would cry with them and then hug them. They all needed God and His love. This is so very hard to convince someone who has been abused. We do not feel that we deserve anything good. Many of us blame ourselves, even if we were children when this happened.

I began to feel their pain. This was difficult for me to understand. I had my own issues to deal with. I did not have time for all of their junk. I began to avoid certain people due to this, especially if I was having a good day. I did not want anything to ruin it.

All of them suffered abuse as children, helpless and trusting children. It is so terrible to have the innocence of a child ripped out. In my opinion, the devil knows this. If he can attack the child with such a force, he will not need to do much more in that person's life. The life that follows will bring death. It will be a trail of addiction, broken relationships, families destroyed, promiscuity, and the victim will then become the abuser.

It is a cycle that will continue to repeat itself until someone stands up and says, "no more." If an individual will turn to the one who created us, and allow Him in to heal, God is more than ready to assist us. After all, He created the universe and all in it.

The major problem is that they are usually mad at God. Some will admit it and others will deny it. We think, "How could He let this happen to me? Where were you when it all happened?" This is a trap from the pits of hell. If the devil can keep us mad at God we will not go to the one who can heal. God is the only one who can bring complete restoration and deliverance.

After God began to heal me from the shame, it was easier to talk about my past. I was able to share what worked and what didn't. I was finally able to realize that it was not my fault, that I did not ask to be raped or molested. I did not cause the problem. When I could separate these things from me, I started to like myself a little bit. I could look in the mirror and not think I was too ugly.

I have heard it said, "When you pray for others' healing, you too will be healed." I have found out that this is true. The more I prayed for others and shared my heart, I was healed, little by little. These individuals took me back to where I needed to go. At times it was so difficult I could barely stand it.

God had to teach me the valuable lesson of release. Sometimes I would feel overburdened. During this time I spoke with my spiritual advisor. He gave me a wonderful piece of advice. He told me how difficult it was at times hearing confessions. He said that many times the sins and burdens were so heavy he could hardly take it.

He explained after hearing confessions, as he took his Stole off, he would also leave the burdens in the confessional. He told me that I would need to leave the burdens at the foot of the cross. Each and every person and burden belonged to the Lord.

The times I spent with my spiritual advisor were special. He was always there to keep me on the right track. He would provide the direction when times were uncertain. Many times I would go the meeting full of anxiety and confusion. I would always leave with clear direction on what Jesus wanted. He would listen when I needed to talk and scold me when I was out of line.

The meetings for me were a lifesaver during very dark times in my life. I wanted to do what Jesus wanted me to do. My spiritual advisor became a dear friend to me. I was able to see Jesus in him. He gave up his life like Jesus did. He was never too busy to spend time with me. The relationship is one that I truly cherish.

I wanted to help others so much that I would hold them in my heart. I wanted to protect them, to keep them from feeling any more pain. I wanted to protect the little children like I had the little girl in me.

God began to show me that by holding on to them I was getting in His way. I had some crazy idea that I could save them. Jesus had to tell me over and over again that He was the only Savior. Pride was attempting to rear its ugly head once again.

At first it was hard for me to let each person go. I had to release each and every person that I had prayed for. Many times it would appear bad things were happening after I let them go. Actually, these events were the very thing that would get them where they needed to be.

I now realize that sometimes we must feel the pain. Many times pain is a motivator for change. I heard a story about Jesus the shepherd. A shepherd may sometimes have to break the leg of a sick sheep, because the sick sheep puts up such a fight. It is when the shepherd breaks the leg; the shepherd can put the sheep over his shoulders.

It is so true for many of us. We put up such a fight that Jesus may need to break our leg in order to carry us. I was the sheep who was still fighting with one broken leg. Jesus had to break both of my legs.

As humans we will do what ever we can to avoid pain. It hurts so badly that we want to run and hide from it in anyway possible. The problem is, that when we run from it, we are also running from God.

Once I could understand this, and accept it in my heart, I was completely able to release. When I released each one, I was allowing the powerful hand of the Lord to move. I prayed for them and then surrendered them to God.

They were free to grow, and free to feel their pain. God can and will turn all things to good if we let Him. He will even take the bad and turn it completely around. If God is capable of creating the entire universe, He is more than qualified to take care of His people.

With all of my heart, I wanted to do something for all of the people who were hurting. I wanted to help in anyway that I could. The call was getting bigger each and every day. The only thing that I could do was to pray. That is what I did, I prayed. I started praying for others and not just myself.

I started to feel a call in my heart. I deep desire which is hard to explain. The things that were once important to me now weren't. I could not understand what was going on with me.

My dream job as a supervisor was no longer giving me the satisfaction that it once did. I started to feel a desire in my heart to help others.

I had no idea what to do next. I kept hearing this voice in my head saying, "If you want to walk on water you have to get out of the boat."

12

Speak out for those who can't speak, for the rights of all the destitute.
(Proverbs 31:8)

The Mission

The call in me was getting bigger every day. The desire to help other victims was getting stronger day by day. At times I was certain that I had lost my marbles. I was sure that I was going crazy. I would pray day after day asking God to remove this from my heart. I did not want to do what He asked, even though I prayed to Jesus back in Medjugorje.

In Medjugorje I went to the risen crucifix and prayed with other pilgrims. I prayed, "Jesus, I am yours; do with me what you will. I give you my hands, I give you my legs, I give you my heart, and I give you my mouth. Jesus I give you all of me." At the time I meant each and every word. I wanted Him to have all of me. Little did I know that He would take me up on my offer and change the course of my life.

Things had been changing in me ever since this prayer. I wanted to go up to the mountains and shout. Jesus is present in our Churches; He is waiting for us at Adoration. He is alive in the presence of the Most Holy Eucharist. He is here, and He was still in the family business.

Jesus is still on this earth carrying on the family name. He is still healing and delivering those oppressed. Only God Himself knows where He has brought me. He knows the pains that were so deep in my hardened heart. God knew all about me and He still wanted to heal me. That was so amazing. How could He love me the way He does?

God had begun a great work. He will do the same for you. All we need to do is, ask, seek and knock. Who would have thought He would heal all of the past. He removed all of the pain, I had tried so very hard to bury.

I have seen many wounded people that God has touched. He has begun to move in such a powerful way. He has healed cancer, addicts, marriages, and brought the prodigals back one by one.

The wonderful news is He is just waiting to heal the wounded and rejected. I finally was able to believe He wanted to heal me. I knew with all of my heart, if I kept His commandments and followed Him, He would be faithful to me, as I was to Him. Many of us believe God is an enforcer or the punisher. We may even believe we have to be all fixed up before we can come to Him. Maybe you are one of those people who think you have to get better and then you can come home.

Maybe this impression has been in you since youth. When you go to church, look around, all come in their Sunday best. They are all cleaned up and have their happy faces on. Yes, it is true that God appreciates each and every one who is there. I remember Jesus saying, "Those who are well have no need of a physician, but those who are sick; I have come to call not the righteous but sinners to repentance." (Luke 5:31-31). The sick are in need of Jesus. I am just so grateful, I am still sick and in need of Him.

What about all of the ones who are not in the Church, the ones who do not feel worthy to be in Church? What impressions do they have of your church? Would they feel welcomed if they came in dirty? How would they be treated? Would you go to welcome them? Would you give them love? Jesus gave a command to the apostles, "This is my commandment, that you love one another as I have loved you." (Matthew 15:12).

Let's look at how Jesus loved. He ate with the tax collectors and the prostitutes. He healed the lepers and those oppressed by the devil. He went out to the caves and brought them out, forgave them, healed them, and loved them. He told them to sin no more. But He loved them, and was treated so poorly because of His love. He was the Son of God sent by His father and did what God wanted Him to do. We all claim to be Christians, to be followers of Christ. We say that we believe all Jesus taught. We are all called to love the unlovable. If we are not doing this, we are not His true disciples.

This message is for all of you. The ones who are suffering silently, who are ashamed and rejected. This is for the tax collectors and the prostitutes. It is for those who suffer from addictions and feel as if they are so unworthy. Jesus Christ of Nazareth came for you. His Father, your Father said, "For a brief moment I abandoned you, but with great compassion I will gather you in overflowing wrath for a moment I hid my face from you, but with everlasting love I will have compassion on you, says the Lord, your Redeemer." (Isaiah 54:7-8). This has got to be the best news you have heard today. He loves you right now. Right where you are, even if you are dirty and rejected. God the Father, The Son and the Holy Spirit love you. They want you to be free and to follow them.

The Mission

The Blessed Mother said at the wedding feast of Canaan, "Do what ever He says." The Blessed Mother is telling us something. We are to do what He says to do: love.

This has become the mission; it will not leave me. I have tried to wish it away and pray it away. My life would have been much easier. I have been misunderstood, talked about, laughed at and made fun of. I have been accused of being crazy, that I have lost it. It still would not leave.

After trying so hard to pray it away, God has put in my heart to write this book. I did not want to do it. I ran for so long. I did not want anyone to know what happened to me. I had made so many promises to myself. I promised to take these things to my grave. The last thing that I ever wanted was to talk about it. I wanted to pretend all was great. I could not imagine what people would think if they knew.

The hardest thing for a victim to do is break the silence. Victims will not even tell those close to them. God had to deal with me for such a long time before I finally gave Him my complete surrender.

I tried to give Him every excuse I could think of. I did not have a college degree, I was off of the hook, I was an alcoholic, I was molested, and I was not a writer. I did not know anything about writing. I was a major sinner and had a colorful past. I had so many problems, who would read it? Over and over I told Him that I was not a Saint but a sinner.

I was so scared to do this. I could not figure out what the big deal was. I remember one day in prayer I said, "God, what is the big deal about this book? Don't people know that you can heal them of this stuff?" I heard a voice in my heart saying, "You didn't, did you?" I began to understand. He was right. I had no idea that God would heal me from the rape. I believed in the healing power of God. I was sure that God could heal those with cancer. I had seen it with my own eyes. I just could not fathom, that He would do anything with my heart. I was resigned to the fact; I would be living with this all of my life. I just had no hope. I accepted my mess and did not dare pray for it to heal.

Jesus has proven to me that He loved me. He came to help me and showed that I would need to do the same for others. I need to spread the good news. He wants us to reach the ones who are still out there. So today, I pray that this book will bring hope. That it will touch at least one heart. I pray that one person will be convinced of the love of God. That maybe, just maybe, you will believe there is hope for you. Even for the ones the world has called hopeless. I pray that you believe you are not hopeless.

When God came into my life, I could not have lived one more moment without Him. I needed help. Dirty and ashamed, I came back to Him. He promised that all things work for the good of those who love Him. That was all I had to give Him. The only thing I had was my love for Him. I have loved Jesus and in turn, He has turned all things to the good.

He carried me many times when I could not walk. He would send me the support when I needed it. He has been so faithful to me during my walk back home to Him.

So, now I will do as Our Lady has said. I will do whatever He says. I owe my life to Jesus. I will do as He has instructed me to do. I will try to go out into the caves and bring out the lepers. I will pray for God to heal and touch in a way He never before has. I pray for each reader to receive the gift of Hope and the gift of Faith. I pray that these pages become a light in your darkness. I pray that somehow, I have been able to tell you about Jesus.

Through these few pages, you can see for yourself, the amazing love that the Father has for His children. Maybe, just maybe, you will begin to believe, if God has healed me, He can do the same thing for you. If God can do something in my life, imagine for a moment what He can and will do for you. The only thing you will need to do is to believe.

I had such a hard time receiving from God. Somewhere deep down inside me, I had believed I was bad. Only someone who was bad would have been molested. Only a bad person would have been raped, and then became a full-fledged alcoholic. This was the hardest thing for me to overcome. I was not a bad person. Bad things may have happened to me, but I was not bad.

I was one of those people who said things like, "What else can happen?" Or "When it rains, it pours." I was walking around claiming bad things. It is no wonder they followed. In the Bible we are told to have faith. Jesus talked about this. The Lord replied, "If you had faith the size of a mustard seed, you could say to this mulberry tree, be uprooted and planted in the sea; and it will obey you." (Luke 17:6) This scripture amazed me. I have seen a mustard seed. It is pretty small, not big at all. I thought about this, prayed, and I realized something: I was negative and did not have any faith.

I had even been walking with God and praying all kinds of prayers. It seemed like when I prayed for others, I could see God move. I had faith when it came to others. When it came to my family, and me I lacked this.

The Mission

I started to pray for the gift of Faith. I needed it so very desperately. My prayers were not moving because I had no faith. I had faith in God. I did not believe for one minute I deserved it.

We go around punishing ourselves for the past. We will not even accept good things. It is hard for us to accept anything good, especially when we are used to bad. This can cause so many problems. We need to pray that God will heal us of this.

God is such a loving Father. He, like any good father, wants to give good things to His children. We just need to learn how to receive. We do not need to jump through hoops or be perfect for God to do these things for us. We need to be obedient and love God. We will fall as all humans do. God is fully aware of our weakness; He created us. When we fall, we need to admit our faults, pick ourselves up and try again.

God is not at all like we are. Humans love conditionally. We will withhold love if someone does not do what we want. God is nothing like that. He will not withhold His love from us, even when we are not perfect. That is so hard for us to accept. We do not need to be perfect to come to God. We can come to Him even if we are dirty. You do not need to wait another moment.

If you have felt anything like I did, you can't stand one more moment in your pit. You need to hear this good news. You do not need to wait. You can come to Him right now. You do not need to wait until you are cleaned up. You do not need to wait until things get a little better. The time is now and the day is today.

I can give you a money-back guarantee. Surrender yourself to God. Allow Him to come in and clean you up. He will give you so much more than you expect. He is the only one to deliver us from the bondage. He is the only answer to your problems. There is no other way to get what He alone can give. The only real peace on this earth can come from Him.

This is the mission: to announce to all of the tax collectors, call out to the lepers, all the sinners, all those who are just like me God will give you that freedom and offer you a new beginning. He promises, "I will repay you for the years that the swarming locust has eaten, the hopper, the destroyer, and the cutter, my great army which I sent to invade you." (Joel 2:25) He said it, I didn't. He came to heal the brokenhearted and bind up the wounds.

Let Him in; open your hearts. Give up your mess and He will give you so much more.

13

And He said to them, "Follow Me and I will make you fish for people." Immediately they left their nets and followed Him. (Matthew 4:19-20)

The Decision

Although I felt the call to help others in my heart, God was waiting for me to make the decision. He was waiting for my fiat. It was something that I had not done yet. I still had free will and the decision was mine. At any time, I had the opportunity to turn back and walk away. I felt the call, but could not imagine how any of it would happen.

I was faced with a dilemma, should I keep this job and have all of the material things? Would I stay so my children could have the best of everything, or would I follow God?

I have heard many people say when God is finished with something you will know. He took His blessing off of this job. It was gone and all that was left was struggle. He took the desire and fun out of the job. He planted a deep desire in its place to be with my family and do His will. The only question was, when would it be and how could it possibly happen? Maybe it was wishful thinking or a fantasy.

My job had become my identity. All of my self-esteem was wrapped up in my position and the money I made. It was very hard to admit, but it was the truth. My job was the one thing in life at which I had been successful. It was one of the hardest things to give up.

I finally agreed to leave. I prayed and told God I would do whatever He wanted. I finally made the decision to give Him back the job He had given me.

During this time my mind was going back and forth. I would try to come up with various reasons why I should stay. I even got to the point where I would be convinced to let go of the idea.

God had a funny way of getting my attention. I will never forget the message at Church one Sunday. I had been praying over my decision and

The Decision

wanted a sign. I sat in Mass and the homily that day was for me. Father said, "When Jesus touches your heart and heals you, it is your duty to go back and help others." Another time, I was at a retreat praying for another confirmation. We were listening to a talk and Father spoke about people doing great things for God. I perked up a bit, he said, "It only takes one person to do something great for God." I had been giving Jesus my excuses of why I could not do what He wanted. The first one was that I was only one person. The next thing I would say was, "Jesus, I am such a sinner. You can not possibly want to use me."

When things were extremely rough, I would start to feel sorry for myself. Just when I was thinking about the mess my life was in, the phone would ring. It would always be someone in need of comfort. I was able to focus on someone other than myself. This helped me to take my eyes off of me and on to them. Many of the people I talked to had problems far bigger than mine.

I was preparing to go on retreat in April. Father Sudac would be back in the States. I had made plans to attend with my children. I was looking forward to this time of prayer. I needed to be filled up again. I was running on empty.

While I was at Adoration, I heard in my heart that I would not be working when I went to the retreat. I sat there and said, "How can this be, the retreat is six weeks away?" There was no way possible. Usually before this happens, we hear rumors. Upper management knows about it and we have time to prepare. I sat there and said, " If you say so." I did not believe it was going to happen.

I waited and waited for this to happen; but nothing did. I felt like a fool. Maybe I was just going crazy; that seemed to be my life these days. I started talking to God. "I can not take any more of this God. I have had it, I am going to walk in there and quit. These people are driving me crazy."

My mind drifted to Abraham and Sara, God had promised them a son. Even though they were too old to have a child. God had told them He would perform a miracle. They waited and waited, and still nothing. Finally Sara was not willing to wait any longer. She took matters into her own hands. Sara had instructed her maid to be with Abraham and she had a son. Sara made a complete mess and had to deal with it. God finally did give them the gift of Isaac. The miracle happened, but not when they thought.

I knew if I took control and quit, I would miss the miracle. I took a deep breath and prayed, "Fine, God, I will wait, but you are going to have to help me." I calmed down and went back in the office. I was able to make it through the day. I was grateful that it was Friday. I would have the weekend to calm down.

By the time Sunday came around I was fine. I was feeling much better. I had accepted the fact that I would be working for now. I was at peace and ready for a new week.

The day started off like every other day. I made my morning rounds, talking to my team. The day would be filled with the normal activities. Conference calls, one-on-one meetings with employees, and "putting out fires" for the day. God had given me a gift over the weekend; I was filled with calmness and a peace. I savored each and every moment of this and enjoyed the day.

Early afternoon the announcement came over the PA system. My boss was calling a meeting. He was requesting all management employees to attend. This was not too abnormal. We were used to meetings. The only thing that was strange was the location. We were to report to a conference room at the other end of the building.

Walking in you could feel the tension. The look on my manager's face told the story. He was worried and it was obvious. He was not good at pretending. At that point I was certain the day had finally arrived. It was finally here. I was not sure if I should jump up or run.

He waited for all of us to get inside before starting. He was not smiling when he spoke. Inside I wanted to scream, my heart was ready to jump out of my chest. Sighing, he started, "Over the weekend all of the managers were called to participate on an emergency call. We were told that we would be having another layoff. The company will be accepting volunteers. If we do not get enough volunteers. We will proceed with the layoffs. All of this would be taking place within the month.

No one was saying a word. We just sat there and looked at each other. I was amazed. I could not believe it, every detail happened. God did speak to me, and I would be done with work in time for the retreat. Five days ago, I sat in my boss's office and he said we would not be having any layoffs. I guess God had other plans.

Something in me changed that afternoon. My faith grew in so many ways. I was sure that God had spoken to me. He did what He said. I found out that God was faithful to His people. He took care of all the details. I have found out, circumstances do not matter to God. If He says it will happen, you had better believe it will.

The Decision

Because I had already prepared for this, I did not need to finish any work. I was organized. The work I needed to complete was minimal. I was able to leave two weeks before the others.

I'd be lying if I told you that I was not afraid. I was terrified and excited. I would have waves of fear rushing over me. I had to believe that, no matter what happened, it was going to be good.

I would go through many tests and trials. It was going to be rough. I had to hold on to God and believe what He said. I had to get out of the boat. At times it was very dark, but something kept me going. I had to remember it is always the darkest just before the dawn.

A new beginning was on the horizon. I felt a freedom I had never felt before. It was a time for change. A new person was about to be born. It was Raquel. A woman, wife, young mother, daughter and friend. She was getting ready to come out of the tomb. A new life was waiting for me. All I needed to do was to walk the rest of the way through the desert.

14

So if anyone is in Christ, there is a new creature: everything old has passed away; see everything has become new. (2 Corinthians 5:17)

Freedom - A New Beginning

R eality set in when I handed my badge and pager to my boss. I made a promise that day. At my next job, I wanted to work where I could spend all day talking about God.

There were many times I was told by my boss that I did not need to be a counselor. I spent too much time with the employees. I had grown to care too much for the people and enjoyed spending time with them. I needed to be more businesslike and less compassionate. Well the compassionate side of me won. I was getting ready to say *adios*.

I walked down the hall for the last time. I had walked this hall hundreds of times before, but it was different this time. I felt like something had died. I was in mourning.

So many emotions ran through me. I was happy, sad, excited, terrified and exhausted. As I drove out of the parking lot tears were streaming down my face. What if I have made a terrible mistake? What if it was not God talking to me? I had to trust in what I believed to be true.

At home things were different. It was not going the way I thought it would. I had a hard time just relaxing. I had gotten used to running all of the time. I had a hard time sleeping. I would wake up early in the morning.

In the morning I started walking since now I had the time. I was feeling like I would explode. I can't tell you the freedom I felt. Most of my life I felt different, that I could not even do normal things. I was afraid to come out. I could not even enjoy something as simple as a walk. This day was different from all the other days. For the first time in my life I felt normal. I finally belonged. I felt like I was human and not an animal that did crazy things. It was awesome!

A week after I was home, I received a phone call from my husband, telling me that the company he worked for was getting ready to go on strike. I sat there speechless. What in the heck was going on? I could not believe it. I was just removed from the payroll. I had no job and no money. I sat there and said, "God what are you doing?" I thought you wanted me to be home. How can I do what you want me to with no money?"

The situation affected both my husband and me. Even though we were not talking about it, we were both concerned. I was at home, and my husband was left to carry the financial burden. It was a time of confusion and doubts.

God knew what He was doing. We needed to go through all of this for healing in our marriage. It was so hard and scary. The amazing thing happened; we grew closer than we had ever been.

Over the years, we had started to drift apart. Like so many other couples, we were living two different lives. We were trying to stay together but were drifting. These difficulties caused us to communicate in ways we never had. We opened up and spoke about things we had never talked about. It was hard time, but a good time. I am a witness that God will use suffering to bring out good. He has done this in my life many times.

We had both been raised in homes where the father was absent. We lived through financial difficulties. We both had the same fear of poverty. This was something that was very difficult for both of us to face. God was patient with us, but He still was making us face this fear.

God had to teach me to not look at the circumstances. This was a difficult test for me. I was convinced I would have roses sent to me when I came home. After all, I made the decision to leave my job. I did this for God. Instead I was given a bunch of thorns.

I wanted to give up so many times. I wanted to run back to what was familiar to me. I wanted to go back to work and make money. I had gotten used to having money in my wallet. I was able to buy whatever I wanted. I was not able to shop the way I used to. My wallet was not as it used to be.

My flesh was screaming. I was being crucified and it hurt. I was not happy about all of this. I was depressed and angry, positive I made a mistake.

Every now and then, I would mention the book to my husband. I am certain he was convinced I was crazy. I had a secret life that I had kept from him. I was so afraid for him to come into it. He fell in love with Rocky, and she did not live in the house any longer. I was afraid he would not like whom I had become, afraid he might run from the new me.

We had spent years partying together. When I changed he lost his buddy. That was hard for both of us. At times I even started to think we had nothing in common. I know he felt the same way. There was major change in our house, and it affected both of us.

I am thankful to God. He has healed the marriage. I remember clearly when God spoke to me. He said, "You need to let your husband into your heart. Just like you did me and Jesus." I sat there speechless I was terrified. I could not believe what He was asking of me. I said to Him, "But God, You guys have never hurt me."

I knew this was not an option for me. It was not a choice but a command. I have learned that, if God tells you to do something, He will give you the grace to do it. It may not be easy it may even hurt. You may not think you are ready. If God says you are ready, trust me you are ready.

I prayed for this and God moved suddenly. He has healed the marriage in so many ways I never dreamt possible. He breathed His life into a dead thing. He raised the marriage from the dead, just like Jesus did with Lazarus.

Jesus heard about the death of his friend. He was called and went to the home. Lazarus had been dead for days. Jesus went there and commanded them to open the tomb. The Bible says that when they rolled the rock back, it smelled. Jesus commanded Lazarus to arise and walk and he did. Jesus can take your old life and raise it from the dead.

God taught me how important my marriage was to Him. He showed me that the covenant among the three of us was very important to Him. My marriage and how I treat my husband matter to God. The book is no good, all of my prayers are no good, if I do not honor the marriage. Before I could write this book, I had to get my house in order. I had to change and love my husband the way God does.

Today my marriage means more to me than anything. God first, Steve second, and the children third and me last. Do you notice who is last? That's right, number one has been moved to last. God has a sense of humor.

I have been humbled in many ways. While I was working, I had this mindset. I would never be caught dead in any clothes from Wal-Mart. My kids were better than that also. After all I worked and we deserved this. That was not good enough for me. If it weren't name brand I would not wear it. I wanted my kids to look great. I wanted them to feel good about themselves. The only thing I created with this attitude was spoiled daughters. Girls who expected to get things.

I was so shallow, concerned only about the outside and not the inside. My children were taught that material things made you a person. We had all gotten to the point of expecting it.

When I came home all of this changed. We all went through the mall withdrawals. We could no longer afford to buy all of the extras. Buying the girls things was my way of making up for what I could not give them. For a long time I could not give them a real mother.

I learned a very important lesson. You do not need material things to make you happy. You can actually be happy with the small things. When you do not need outside things to make you happy, God can give them to you. I believe it is okay to have nice things. God wants to bless His children. He will prepare us for the blessing, testing us to see the motive. He needs to make sure we can handle the blessing.

Wal-Mart is now my favorite store; I actually wear clothes from there. When we shop now, it is different. We have learned to appreciate the things we get. I was given a gift and I am thankful.

I used my time by going to the girls' ball games. I looked forward to the next softball or tee-ball game, all the various sporting events that the kids participated in. It was special to share this with my children.

We all enjoyed this time together. The best part was when one of the girls hit the ball. She would run to first base and look to see if I was watching. Our eyes would meet and then came the thumbs up. This made them smile and it was a gift. It was good for both of us. They were looking for my acceptance and they got it. On the ride home we would talk about the game and discuss various plays. This was priceless; I could not buy this in a mall. It brought us closer.

Many times I wondered how they felt when I worked. Who were they looking for when I was not there? Whose eyes were there for them? I know it had not been mine I was too busy working.

Parents, you must realize the importance of supporting your children. They want only your love and acceptance. Maybe you were like me, wanting to give them material things, to provide a nice life for them. You want to make sure they have more than you did as a child. What are you giving up when you do this? Can you go back and give them what they want more than anything else? Children need their parents. They need you! Money can't buy the time you spend with your children. That will make them confident and secure. Pray and see what God wants.

I want to bring up a word of caution. You may be excited today; maybe you have hope where there was only despair. You may even believe that God can and will heal you. Do not go looking for it. Do not try to dig for anything. When God is ready to heal you, He will bring up things to you;

He will lead you step by step in this process. He will direct your steps and hold your hand.

I also want to talk about obedience. You can't expect God to come in your life and heal you if you are not willing to do what He tells you to. "Has the Lord as great delight in burnt offerings and sacrifices, as in obedience to the voice of the Lord? Surely, to obey is better than sacrifice, and to heed than the fat of rams." (1 Samuel 15:22) If God is telling you to quit drinking, do not go into the bar. If He is telling you to apologize, do not make any excuses, just do it. He will give you the grace to do it if you cooperate with Him.

Don't be on the fence, trying it sometimes and when you want to have fun, going back to your old ways. It will never work!

God gave Moses the Ten Commandments for a reason. He was not trying to be mean, only to help us. Discipline is a good thing. The Bible even says so, "My child, do not despise the Lord's discipline or be weary of His reproof, for the Lord reproves the one He loves, as a father the son in whom He delights." (Proverbs 3: 11-12). All I can say is that He must really love me. I can't get away with anything. Don't be like me. I prayed the prayers and then freaked out. Things started to change. For every temptation He provides a way out. That is a promise.

My life is far from perfect; sometimes it is just difficult. The one thing for sure is that my life has changed. The mess is out and there is something beautiful in its place. I now have peace, love and true happiness.

My love for God, Jesus and the Holy Spirit, along with my faith, are growing. He has given me a new beginning. I had to open my mouth and break the code of silence. I was terrified; Jesus sent His Mother to help me. They have been so kind and gentle.

There was a time when my mom told me that I had another mom. My mom was in the bath and I was outside talking to her. She said, "You know Raquel, you have another mother." I started to cry. I said to her, "You mean I am not your daughter? I am adopted, dad is not my dad." She said, "No honey you are not adopted. Your other mom is Mother Mary." Grateful I was not adopted, I looked at her and said, and "I know that mom."

I have never forgotten this. I was able to give myself to my other mom. I made a consecration to the Blessed Mother and can feel her close to me. Thank you, Mom, for the news I had another mom. And thank you, Blessed Mother, for being a wonderful mother. I love you both!

15

You will know the truth and the truth will make you free.
(John 8:32)

Breaking the Silence

There is a secret code, an unwritten rule. You do not have to be threatened to keep silent. You just know: do not talk about it. One never dares to speak about such things. What will others think about me? That is what I thought for so long. I was afraid people would think badly about me. So I, like so many others, kept this code of silence.

There have been victims who have come forward, rape victims who went to court. Many times the victims who broke the code had to pay. They have to pay a price for coming forward. Before it is all said and done, the victim has been put on trial. What message are we sending to victims? In my opinion we are telling them it is far better to keep silent. If we are here to help the victims, why do we allow this to happen?

The act of abuse leaves so many scars. The shame that is attached to these things at times can be unbearable. We need to create a safe environment for those who come forward. They deserve to feel safe and protected. Victims are wounded beyond comprehension and then left with all the dirt.

What are they to do? What are we to do? Who can help these lost and wounded individuals? I have the answer: His name is Jesus Christ of Nazareth. He already knows all about you. He is aware of every pain and every wound. He knows what you have done and what you will do. The good news is, He still loves and accepts you. Jesus said, "And you will know the truth, and the truth will make you free." (John 8:32). It is only the truth, when it is brought to Calvary, that can set you free. This truth has the ability to heal you. You can not escape this or go around it.

The truth, no matter how ugly, will bring freedom. If you do not face the truth, I can promise you one thing, nothing will change. You will wake up tomorrow still feeling the same way. You will continue to remain the prisoner. Life will go on and you will continue to do the same destructive things. You will remain in your cave with no light, only the darkness that surrounds you.

There is no miracle cure from abuse. If so, I have not found it. It requires prayer, obedience, forgiveness and often Christ-based counseling. You have to walk back through it and face the pain. You do not have to go there alone. Jesus is waiting to walk with you into the darkness. He will go into your tomb. He will wait in the dark with you until your resurrection. He will be there with you to help.

I am not an expert in this field. You do not have to listen to one word that I have written. I am not a counselor nor do I hold any college degree. What I have to offer you is the voice of someone who knows your pain. I understand what it is like to live with abuse. I understand the struggles you have and the hopelessness you feel. I have been where you are and now I am able to live.

You may even be one of millions who have been in counseling. One of the supposed survivors. I have a question for you. Is it still in you? Does your abuse still affect your life and the choices you make?

Only God can touch a heart. He created all of us and our hearts. God is the only hope for your heart to be healed. You can sit on a couch year after year and still feel the same inside. God the Father and the Son will heal your broken heart. He promised this. God said, "The Spirit of the Lord is upon me because He has anointed me to bring good news to the poor. He has sent me to proclaim release to the captives and recovery of sight to the blind, to let the oppressed go free." (Luke 4:18)

I do not have the magic answer, but I can share things that have helped me become free. I pray that these pages will become an inspiration for you. I pray for each person who will read this book. I pray that God the Father will shake you and awaken something deep in you heart. I pray that He will touch you in a way He never has before. I pray that Our Father will give you a spirit of Hope. I pray He will shine His light into the dark places of your heart.

I have said this so many times before. "If God can do something with me, He can do something with anyone." Pray for this and allow God to lead and guide you. Open your heart to God and allow Him in. You do not need to protect yourself from God. I promise you He will not hurt you.

God came into my life and he worked all things for my good, just like He promised. I thank God for going through everything. I would not change a thing.

Breaking the Silence

I am going to let you in on a little secret. God can heal you from the rape, rejection, addiction, molestation, hatred, and shame. It is so amazing but true. He has never stopped. He has been doing the same thing since the creation.

God has taken me into the darkness and carried me into His healing light. If you think you are a lost cause, you need to think again. It is written, "God on purpose chooses the weak and foolish things of the world to confound the wise." (1 Corinthians 1:27)

I believe that Our Father is tired of His little ones being hurt. He is getting ready to lead them out of Egypt, as in the Old Testament. He is preparing a mass exodus from Egypt. I believe that God wants to set us free.

Remember one thing: the Israelites had to walk through the desert. It is in the desert where He will heal us. In the desert God will prepare us and test us. It is always the darkest just before dawn.

The Roman Catholic Church is still very much alive. We have so many treasures in our beautiful Church. We have the Sacraments to assist us and strengthen us. We have the greatest gift of all, the true presence of Jesus Christ. We can receive Him each and every day if we choose. Jesus is alive and in the flesh. He is waiting for each one of us in tabernacles, alone many hours of the day. If we truly believed that Jesus is waiting for us, we would all be running to Church to receive the Healer. He is waiting for us to heal our hearts.

At the last supper Jesus gave instructions to his Apostles. He said, "Do this in memory of me." The Roman Catholic Church is doing this each and every day. No matter what country in the world you go to, the Catholic Church is still doing this in memory of Him. This, my friends, is the truth.

No longer do you have to fight. This fight is not your fight, it has already been won. Jesus defeated the enemy on Calvary. It was the Precious Blood of Jesus that was shed for you. He did this for you and for me. Read about His passion, pray for the gift of understanding.

This is the greatest love story ever told. The love God the Father has for each one of us. He gave up His only Son for you and me. Please do not allow His death to be in vain. Accept this message, and sit back and receive it. Jesus died for us to be free. "But He was wounded for our transgressions, crushed for our iniquities; upon him was the punishment that made us whole, and by His bruises we are healed." (Isaiah 53:5.)

My Daddy Never Died

After the death of my father, I felt emptiness. I always thought it would be there. During this journey something awesome happened. The hole is gone and there is something beautiful in its place. I have come to realize my daddy never died. He has always been with me and never left me. I have a Father who is very much alive. His name is Abba. I always knew I was born into royalty. I am the daughter of the King of Kings, God the Father. You see my daddy is still with me. I belong to God and I am His daughter.

Today I pray that you make a decision. Decide to break the code of silence. It is well worth it. I love you, each and every one of you. You are all so special. I know how you feel and I still love and accept you. My Daddy accepts you.

God Bless!

Afterword

I would not feel right if I did not include the most important part of the book. I wanted to take this time and speak about all of the priests who have helped me on this journey. They are the true apostles of Jesus Our Lord and Savior.

Jesus came to the earth to show us how to live. He came and lived, loved, healed, delivered and went to the Cross. He came and instructed His disciples to start a new Church. The Roman Catholic Church is what He taught His apostles. This Church was started by St. Peter. He is the one Jesus gave the keys to. St. Peter, like so many others, died for this Church.

Today the Church lives on; we have the apostles still among us. They are our anointed ones, our beloved priests. We can not forget this. We are honored to be in the presence of a priest. They are Jesus' disciples who have continued in the ministry.

During these dark times when the media speak about our priests, we need to come forward and love them. I am not going to say what happened is fine. I will say the opposite; it is never acceptable when an individual is victimized. Not by anyone including a priest.

I was not hurt by a priest. God used many of His beloved priests to help me. They were there to help me and to pray for me and teach me about the love of Jesus. We need to talk about these priests. We all should be proud to walk down the streets with one of our priests; they deserve it. Our priests have given up their lives to carry on the message of Christ.

I thank God; He has sent me some very special and holy priests. I would like to take a moment to thank each and every one of you. Father Phister, Fr. Sapp, Fr. Kaycee, Fr. Sudac, Fr. Jim Livingston, Fr. Rookey, Fr. Clement Machado, Fr. Bernardin, Fr. Bob, Fr. Abraham, Fr. Whalen, Fr. Hampsch, Fr. DeGrandis, Fr. Koons, Fr. Traub, Fr. Ivan, Bishop John D'Arcy and Fr. Bob Schulty. There are so many of you I could write a chapter about you. Many of Jesus' apostles have been there to help me along this journey. I could not have made it without each and every one of you. Each of you has been a precious gift to me. You have all helped me when I wanted to give up. All of you taught me the gift of self-sacrifice and love. Through you I have seen the love Christ has for his sheep.

We need to remember God can heal through His priests. He will do some powerful things at the hands of His apostles. They are anointed to carry on the ministry of Jesus. If we allow it, God will use each one of them to assist us in life.

They are special and deserve to be treated as such. We take and take from them and expect they will not tire. Our priests are people, too. They are human and get lonely. They need our love, support and friendship.

To those of you have been hurt by a priest, I would like to say one thing. I do not understand exactly how you must feel. I do however understand what you have been left with. The pain, humiliation and shame. I want to tell you, all priests are not like the one who hurt you. In life we have good and evil. You can not allow the evil that wounded you, to keep you from the Church that can heal you.

Thank you, all of my beloved priests. You have all been so wonderful to me. You have been the tools God used to heal me. I love each and every one of you. I pray for you every day. You gave up your lives for us. You have all been wonderful shepherds of the flock.

I can honestly say I have never felt better in my life. God has done something so beautiful in my heart. No one can take this from me. It has been a difficult and long journey. One I will never regret.

I pray, God will touch your heart, that He will give you a desire to ask for a healing. I was so much like St. Mary Magdalene. Jesus delivered her from seven demons. She followed Him for the rest of His life. St. Mary Magdalene was at the foot of the Cross. She was there for Him even unto death. She was not off hiding somewhere. She loved Jesus and stayed with Him until the end.

When Jesus resurrected she was the first one to see Him. To me that says something. Jesus loved her and she was a sinner. I too am a sinner, but I know Jesus loves me.

I want to spread the good news to all sinners just like me. I know there are many more of you out there. I pray this book will give you courage to come out into the light. Thank you, Jesus, for the love you have for me. Thank you, St. Mary Magdalene, for the hope you have given me. Thank you, Heavenly Father, for your mercy.

I completed this book exactly three years to the day, when I came back from Medjugorje, August 6th. The Feast day of the Transfiguration. I do not think it was a mistake. I wanted to finish it August 5th. God as usual had other plans.

May God the Father bless and keep each and every one of you.

Raquel Hanic